Portal
in
Pensacola

The Real Thing Hits Brownsville

Renee DeLoriea

Revival Press

An Imprint of
Destiny Image® Publishers, Inc.
P.O. Box 310
Shippensburg, PA 17257-0310

ISBN 1-56043-189-X

First Printing: 1997   Second Printing: 1997

For Worldwide Distribution
Printed in the U.S.A.

This book and all other Destiny Image, Revival Press,
and Treasure House books are available
at Christian bookstores and distributors worldwide.

For a U.S. bookstore nearest you, call **1-800-722-6774**.
For more information on foreign distributors,
call **717-532-3040**.
Or reach us on the Internet:
http://www.reapernet.com

Dedication

To Susan Wesler, my true friend, who has been there for me every inch of the way with spiritual eyes to see and to confirm, and with a humble heart of constant support, reassurance, wisdom, boldness, and honesty.

Acknowledgments

To my children, Aaron, Rachel, and Aimee, who warm my heart every minute of every day. To my father, Thomas DeLoriea, for teaching me bravery even as a child, and to his wife, Dorothy, who always listened without judgment. To my mother, Linda DeLoriea, who told me about Jesus as a child and reminded me as an adult that I was never alone.

To Pastor John Kilpatrick for having the boldness to be the mouthpiece of God at any cost, for letting God be God, and for protecting and fighting for a sheep like me.

To Stephen Hill for encouraging intercession, for moving with the flow of the Spirit of God, and for toiling unceasingly in the harvest field.

To my brothers and sisters in Christ at Brownsville Assembly of God, for laughing and crying with me, for encouraging me, for praying for me, for warring with me, and for seeking the face of God with me without compromise.

Contents

Foreword

As soon as the revival broke out on Father's Day of 1995, we realized that a strategy must be developed to facilitate what God was doing. One plan was to schedule Friday night baptism services for the new converts and repentant backsliders. What I enjoy so much about the baptisms is listening to sheep talking to other sheep from the baptism pool. Each shares his or her testimony and victories. Nothing else is quite so moving. They have a different perspective and language, one that other sheep can identify with.

In her book *Portal in Pensacola*, Renee DeLoriea approaches the Brownsville Revival from the perspective of a sheep. She gives a refreshing yet journalistic interpretation of what she has seen and experienced. I have witnessed a remarkable change in Renee and her family; they have been impacted in life-changing ways.

I have enjoyed reading the account of the revival from Renee's interpretation. As you read this book, it will help you to catch a glimpse of this mighty move of God and to eavesdrop on some of the inspiring stories.

John Kilpatrick, Pastor
Brownsville Assembly of God Church

Introduction

I have been given the opportunity and privilege of being called to one of the greatest revivals of this century, the Brownsville Revival in Pensacola, Florida. Indeed, God called me to this great move of His Spirit almost seven years to the day before I first walked into His presence at Brownsville. Even though I had lost my way somewhere during my years of spiritual famine, even though I was running away from Him as fast as I could, God drew me back to Him and to the plan He had for my life. He drew me to the mighty revival where He had chosen to share His glory. There He stretched out His mighty hand and washed me in the precious blood of Jesus Christ. He lifted me out depression, defeat, loneliness, oppression, fear, and despair.

The purpose of this book is to show how Jesus filled my heart with consuming love for Him. So many people, from every corner of the world, are crying from deep within, "Please God, there must be more!" By God's grace, I am here to tell you, "Yes, there is more. There is more than you could ever dream possible. I am living it!"

This is a story of the revival of my heart, but it is also the story of Brownsville Revival through my eyes. It is an account of how God has touched me—and hundreds of thousands of others just like me.

Chapter 1

The Assembling of
God's Last-Days Army

Hundreds of pastors and their wives stood on the platform, tears streaming down their cheeks. Some cried uncontrollably. Thousands of hands were stretched toward them as we all prayed that God would spread revival fire to their churches, communities, and lands.

When a missionary to the Ukraine began to testify of his faith that God was going to move in Russia, tears of intercession began to stream from the eyes of believers throughout the sanctuary. As tears welled up in my own eyes, I heard people crying to the left of me, then in the middle of the room, then to the right. Finally, hundreds in every direction were weeping in intercession. When the missionary to the Ukraine burst into tears himself, I put my hand over my heart—as if to keep it from breaking. The burden I was experiencing for the lost and hurting around the world was almost greater than my spirit could bear.

Over 3,000 of us stretched our hands toward these men and women of God and prayed. As we prayed, our faith was ignited. We knew God was about to do something powerful. He saw the tears, He heard our cries, and He saw our faith. He would respond by moving like never before.

No one seemed able to restrain the flood of tears as we pleaded with God to spread revival fire across the world. My own heart began to break as these ministers reached their hands toward heaven and sang, "Revival fire fall, revival fire fall! Fall on us here with the power of Your Spirit, Father let revival fire fall."[1] I made my way to the altar. The closer I drew to where these ministers stood, the harder I cried for all they had endured, all they were about to endure, and all they were willing to endure. I cried without inhibition for the millions of lives that desperately need to be touched by our merciful Lord and Savior, Jesus Christ. As we began to sing again, I thought of the thousands of ministers who had left the Brownsville Revival the day before with a fresh anointing from God. I wondered what God was doing in their churches and in the lives of the persons around them.

Pastor Kilpatrick announced that he had a burden from God for these ministers who had come to Brownsville that week. Therefore, he wanted them to immediately begin to use the new anointing God had given them. He encouraged them to go out in the congregation and begin praying for people. As about 100 very determined and equipped soldiers of the cross filed past me, I saw right into their eyes. I knew our prayers had been answered when they descended rapidly from the platform, set in motion with sound purpose and adamant confidence. Look out, powers of doubt and darkness, the troops are mighty and are on the move!

I moved a few steps back into the congregation area and waited for a minute for a pastor's wife to pray for me. An elderly pastor had already prayed for me as he came off the platform. When he cupped my head between both of his hands I immediately felt a powerful anointing of God and fell under the power of the Holy Spirit. Now I wanted more of Him, and I wasn't ashamed of it. As I waited, I watched a spiritually equipped brigade of pastors and their wives literally march all over the sanctuary; people were quickly being slain in the Spirit before them as they prayed for one person after another and another. People got up off the floor after being slain in the Spirit filled with such a spirit of joy and exhilaration that nearly a thousand people were joyfully dancing and singing before the Lord while others ran to line up for more prayer. I was reminded of the Scriptures that speak of people leaping and praising God.

I saw the Ukrainian missionary praying for people down in the altar area just under the pulpit. I half-skipped, half-ran over to him for prayer. As I watched the missionary gently and tenderly pray for others, countless numbers of people danced, sang, and prayed in the altar area. My heart was struck with a worshipful thankfulness to God for all those rejoicing whom I had personally seen accept Jesus Christ into their lives over the past year. I thought, *It's hard to believe this is really happening.* Many of these precious children of God had once been on drugs, in depression, or broken and tattered in one way or another, yet God had miraculously drawn them to the revival and mercifully washed them in the blood of Jesus Christ! He had set them free and restored them by His Spirit—just like He had done for me. Now we were all together taking part in one of this century's greatest celebrations in God. None of us deserved to be there. It was all due to the grace of God and the power and tender mercy of our beautiful Savior.

I looked up and saw Pastor Kilpatrick pacing back and forth across the platform, making sure we were all okay. Evangelist Steve Hill stood off to the side, taking it all in with a large grin on his face. There were many others around me in the crowd who had comforted me and prayed for me during all the months of growing pains and joy. Once again, all I could do was cry and thank God for bringing me home.

Committed and Commissioned

It had started the first night of the November 1996 Pastors' Conference at Brownsville Assembly of God in Pensacola, Florida. I walked into the sanctuary filled with the great expectation of the 2,000 pastors and their spouses who were assembled there. They had come from every state in the nation and from the far corners of the earth. At last, there seemed to be hope for a real move of God—the kind of move they had dreamed about, the kind of move they had read about in history books and in Scripture. A portal, a grand opening in the heavens, had sovereignly opened over Pensacola, and the *shekinah* glory of God was streaming down upon His people like rays of brilliant sunshine piercing the clouds of an abating thunderstorm.

These men and women of God seemed to be wondering if it might be possible that God would actually give them just a little bit of the anointing they had heard God was pouring out at Brownsville. Earlier in the day I had heard many of them say that they were feeling beat up, worn out, and war torn from the hardships and heartaches of ministry. They were hungry for God to move in their lives and in their ministries. Eager and apprehensive hearts seemed to be saying, "God, in Joel 2:28-29 You promised

You would pour out Your Spirit on all flesh. Could it really be possible that 'all flesh' may actually include me and those I have prayed over and poured my life into for all of these years?"

Most of the people in that room could have easily echoed the words of Pastor John Kilpatrick of Brownsville Assembly of God, "That beast of religion that we rode for so long finally dumped us off in the middle of a big, dry desert where we found ourselves so thirsty and so hungry for the things of God that we thought we were about to die." Pastor Kilpatrick also described their reason for coming to Pensacola: "God has sovereignly decided to once again replenish the parched, dry places of our hearts and lives. By His grace and mercy, He has sent in a river, and in that river is His glory, His manifest presence, and the things of God that we, for such a long time, have longed for and yearned for and cried for."

Just like he often does during revival services where he and Evangelist Steve Hill encourage ministers and others who have made the long journey to Pensacola, Pastor Kilpatrick gave further assurance that God would move in the lives of these men and women in a personal and miraculous way: "The anointing God has poured out here is a transferable anointing. God sees your hunger and thirst for Him. Your hunger and thirst is evidenced by the fact that you have made the pilgrimage here, and God will most assuredly fill you."[2]

The atmosphere that Tuesday night was charged with anticipation and wonder. Every pew was filled with ministers and wives dressed in their Sunday best. Folding chairs were inched into every square of available space. Just being anywhere on the campus seemed to be a relief to these individuals, but those who had found themselves a place somewhere in the sanctuary let out squeals of joy and sighs of relief. They acted a bit like they had unexpectedly and undeservedly discovered a pot of heavenly gold dust.

Most had obviously heard how, day after day, 3,000 to 5,000 people lined up with their lawn chairs and umbrellas, waiting up to ten hours in the hot sun, driving rain, or damp cold in hopes of getting a seat in the sanctuary for one of the revival services. That night, the thousands of ministers and others who were watching by large-screen, closed-circuit television in the chapel, cafeteria, or choir room were also happy to have a seat at all, for reserved space in the conference had been completely full for over two months.

The glorious presence of God's Spirit had long since broken down denominational barriers during those first 17 months of the Brownsville Revival. When God shows up, man-made barriers and opinions quickly seem to fall to the wayside. For instance, one night I witnessed a Methodist minister and a Pentecostal deacon labor together to baptize new converts. Later I saw an Episcopalian woman on the Brownsville prayer team lay hands on and pray for a Baptist preacher and his wife. This night was no different: It seemed that almost every denomination was represented in some way. Ministers, with backgrounds as varied as Baptist, Assembly of God, Methodist, Presbyterian, Quaker, Pentecostal Holiness, and Lutheran, were all crammed into their seats like dressed-up sardines...or could it be that they were more like fine powder that was about to be fragranced by the presence and the anointing of God?

When the service began, hundreds of volunteer conference workers thankfully settled into their metal folding chairs in the tent that had been set up for them in the parking lot. All week these volunteers had been bustling about, telling us all how privileged and honored they felt about being given the opportunity to be a part of, and actually work in, such a powerful move of the Spirit of God—a move of God that was about to touch the nations of the world through this congregated core of ministers! Those of us who had worked many long days and nights in preparation for and in anticipation of the arrival of these many ambassadors of the gospel felt quite light on our feet and fluttery in our hearts because we could almost feel God smiling at us. We knew He was pleased to see so many so hungry for a touch from Him! Part of our glow came from our sneaking suspicion that God was smiling on His laborers at Brownsville too.

Evangelist Steve Hill often quotes Leonard Ravenhill, saying, "The opportunity of a lifetime must be seized during the lifetime of the opportunity." All of us were doing just that. Just as over 75,000 souls had seized the opportunity of being saved and set free by Jesus Christ at the Brownsville Revival during the past 17 months, we, on that night, were seizing the opportunity of being a part of what God is doing in these last days. We were all, in our own way and in our varying degrees of faith, believing God to send revival rain into lives, churches, and communities around the world.

I think we were each somehow assured that we would in some way be individually used in this latter-day great awakening, the glow of which we had particularly begun to see during the past few months. Reports were coming back to Pensacola in increasing and surprising proportions of how God was beginning to pour out revival power in many parts of the world as ministers and laypeople returned from Brownsville to their hometowns and homelands across the nation and world. Those of us working as volunteers in the revival and in the conference agreed that we were, and are, willing to do whatever it takes to contribute to giving glory to God and be of service to our brethren and mankind, whether our part was to scrape plates and scrub toilets for God's ministers or witness at the local burger place. We knew God would be honored by our hearts and our sacrifices made for Him regardless of how large or small the task might appear to be.[3]

The choir sounded the very first note, and on cue, all of us eagerly snapped to our feet. This was it! The battle against the powers of darkness had begun, and in the name of Jesus Christ we had already won! Faith surpassed faith with each new song of victory, hope, and prayer. Songs of praise and of expectation of the soon-to-return Bridegroom Jesus Christ set our feet to dancing. Songs of worship melted our hearts before our mighty Creator and merciful Savior. Songs of prayer for our country ignited patriotic prayer for our land and for the homelands of others. Songs of family and of God the Father's love brought us all to tears. And songs of revival fire filled our hearts with a steadfast faith that our melodic prayers were surely being answered in that very moment. In spite of all the revival services I had been in, I had never before felt such a powerful unity of faith and corporate determination to receive from God and to fulfill His will. I felt that if a mountain had stood before us, it would have surely melted right there. The men and women gathered together in that moment represented the very pillars of God's Church. I really sensed that after a week of corporate prayer and individual refreshing and anointing, nothing would stand a chance of getting in their (or our) way of doing exploits for the Kingdom of God.

Drawn to God's Glory

Suddenly Pastor Kilpatrick announced that 25 or so church neighbors and passers-by had been drawn to the tent in the parking lot and had joined the conference volunteers in singing praises to God in unison with the service in the sanctuary through the closed-circuit television. Steve Hill had often said that he couldn't wait until the manifest presence and glory of the Lord would go beyond the church walls and supernaturally draw people in who were passing by the church. This was the first time overflow services had been held in a tent outside the church, and it was truly a milestone marker of the fulfillment of this prophecy, or prayer. Many of us grinned at each other and shook our heads in amazement at how God never ceases to surprise us with His faithfulness and His providential ways. Many of the curious visitors also received Jesus Christ as their personal Savior that night.

With the lights still dimmed, someone began running through the aisles holding up the beautifully tapestried "Souls" banner while 15-year-old Charity James belted out the song, "Run to the Mercy Seat"—just as she had done during close to 400 revival meetings. As the eight-foot banner streamed and shimmered over people's heads through aisle after aisle, shouts of praise and dances of victory burst out everywhere in the church. Many of us looked at each other wide-eyed as if to say, "Now that's what I call powerful!"

After a couple more songs and a few words of welcome and encouragement, everyone was told it was time to take a "seven and three-quarter" minutes break. First-time visitors to the revival are always surprised that there is a break in the middle of the service. But usually about four hours into the service, they realize the necessity of it. And much to their surprise, the Spirit of God doesn't leave just because we got up for a few minutes to go to the bathroom.

Pastor Kilpatrick's message that night challenged us all to do a thorough housecleaning of our homes, our lives, our relationships, and our attitudes. He warned against the spiritual leprosy of sin and the magnets of demonic oppression that may be allowed to permeate our lives through the television, music, books, relationships, worldly deceptions, and watered-down doctrines concocted by flesh. He also explained how this spiritual leprosy seals off our lives, our homes, and our ministries from the glory of God as the heavens become "brassed over" (turned to brass) by sin. As a result, the flow of God's gifts into our lives becomes hindered or halted. He challenged us to be brave for the cause of holiness and to be bold in the face of persecution and adversity. He rallied us to battle for holiness, not only in our own lives, but in those of our children and families.

Few were left in their seats when the altar call was given. Pastor Kilpatrick asked for all to come forward who had leprosy in their homes, hearts, or ministries. Most of the ministers and their wives lunged to the altar without the least hesitation. It was obvious that revival needed to start with them, with their own commitment to holiness.

Freed to Worship and Rejoice

Thursday night was a night of breaking free in the Spirit as many busted out of their shells of reserve and jumped up and down or danced before the Lord. Pastor Kilpatrick jogged back and forth across the stage; Steve Hill hopped from one foot to the other and spun around with a big smile on his face; Dr. Michael Brown jumped up and down and grinned from ear to ear like a kid who was about to open his first Christmas present; and Brother Dick Reuben shifted from one foot to the other as his big hands clapped to the time of the music. The freedom to rejoice through dancing about a bit, hopping, or whatever seemed to fit, broke loose with Pastor's encouragement and with the song, "Look What the Lord Has Done."

On the first note of that song I jumped from my seat and made my way into the middle aisle where there was still some room. I was glad that so many in the congregation were beginning to feel comfortable to freely express their praise and joy after the two days of anointed sessions with God-picked featured speakers and glorious services.

Pastor Kilpatrick had been sure to tell everyone that this was not a "how to have revival in your church" conference. Rather, it was simply an opportunity for Brownsville to pour out love upon God's ministers so they could receive and take home a fresh anointing. Each featured speaker emphasized that they did not how to "do" revival, but that they had simply learned to let God have His way and to not try to stop or interrupt the flow of what He was doing. The speakers shared what they had experienced in their own lives and in their ministries. This breaking in the Spirit into greater freedom and expression was just another example of letting the Spirit move and have His way. Once again I felt God was smiling.

I drifted over to the aisle left of the platform. I discovered many of my teammates from the Brownsville Revival prayer team were there just having a "good old time" rejoicing, hopping around, and singing about all the Lord has done. After grinning at each other about how tickled we were about the whole thing, I returned my thoughts to God and to rejoicing in all that He has done for me. I couldn't help but notice how happy Pastor Kilpatrick and Steve seemed. After the music stopped, Dr. Michael Brown (otherwise endearingly known at the revival as the "dancing bear") asked the question, "How can we *not* be so happy about all that God is doing that we hop around, and dance, and jump up and down?" It sure made sense to me.

Friday night was a night of intense worship. Although a lot of the songs were pretty upbeat, I just could not keep from bowing my head. It was as though the weight of the glory of God was manifesting His presence and His holiness. One Asian woman testified in broken English from the baptismal pool, "No more Buddha. Buddha never did nothing for me. Jesus do everything for me." Steve was probably the first to jump to his feet. The whole crowd leaped up and shouted praises and declarations of victory.

The testimonies of those set free from dead and hypocritical religion and of those set free from drugs and alcohol warmed and filled our hearts with awe and wonder at God's transforming power. One young teenager testified that he had been raised in Brownsville Assembly but that he had been lusting after girls and was now repenting and giving his all to God. Many shook their heads at this confirmation of the extensive work of holiness and honesty that God was doing in the lives of both the young and the old.

That night, hundreds immediately responded to the altar call. I had been outside of the sanctuary reconciling the accounts for magazine subscriptions, so when I came in the side door to join the altar worker team, hundreds had already come and were on their knees at the altar. I felt blessed to be standing there witnessing the work of God.

Witnessing the Fruit of Revival

Steve called about 12 young people onto the platform. They had been out witnessing on the streets and had won 26 people to the Lord that night. These young people, who go out almost every night, had brought back their sheaves with them. A young black man who received Jesus Christ that night came and stood on the platform with them. Many of these street evangelists had only been serving the Lord for a few months. However, they could each testify to the Scripture: "He that goeth forth and weepeth, bearing precious seed, shall doubtless come again with rejoicing, bringing his sheaves with him."[4]

Steve asked Lindell Cooley, Brownsville's music director, to play a particular song. While we began to sing the familiar Christmas carol, Steve prompted everyone to ask the person next to them if they needed to come to the altar. He explained that some of the most dramatic conversions have taken place when neighbors had asked one another that question. As we all sang the words, "Oh, come all ye faithful, joyful and triumphant," my heart nearly burst with thankfulness to God. I experienced a sense of watching myself from a distance as I stood among so many there at the altar of this history-making, last-days revival, singing with all my heart about the joy and magnificence of the birth of our Savior and Lord. The fact that it was November added to the transparent tenderness, splendor, and illumination of the moment, for we knew this moment would change even our perspective of the approaching Advent season. People of all shapes, sizes, colors, and dress seemed to come out of the woodwork to make their way to the altar. There was a steady stream from every area of the sanctuary. Everyone around me was crying. Some were wailing in repentance at my feet.

God is so amazing and so wonderful. Just when we think it couldn't possibly get any more powerful, it always does! We continued to sing, and more and more people came forward, Pastor Kilpatrick seemed hard-pressed to contain his joy. Lindell looked stunned. Michael Brown marched in place as though he was interceding and doing the walking for those yet to come forward. Steve pleaded with any who might be straggling or holding back: "What are you waiting for? Spend this Christmas season with Jesus in your heart and in your life. Don't let another holiday season go by without Him. Don't let another day go by without Him." People made their way down to the altar so quickly while we sang and cried that I doubted if anyone could possibly resist the wooing of the Holy Ghost. I praised God for calling so many to Himself, just as He had called me to be part of His work here in Pensacola.

Endnotes

1. Paul Baloche, "Revival Fire Fall," Copyright © 1996, Integrity's Hosanna! Music/ASCAP.

2. "Blessed are they which do hunger and thirst after righteousness: for they shall be filled" (Mt. 5:6).

3. "He that is faithful in that which is least is faithful also in much" (Lk. 16:10a).

4. See Psalm 126:6.

Chapter 2

The Call to Azusa Street: Pensacola, Florida

All around me in that airport in Wichita, Kansas, people were looking at me strangely, but I knew the force backing me into that wall was the power of God. I had been walking down the corridor, minding my own business, when an incredible force pushed me backward—like a feather being swept by a strong wind. I had to obey. My muscles fell limp like spaghetti, and when I finally hit the wall, I felt almost weightless. I tried to brace myself by leaning on the wall for support, but again that same powerful force began pushing me sideways to the floor. I thought, *Oh great, I bet those people are **really** looking now.* As I was pushed farther and farther to the floor, God spoke to my spirit in an almost audible voice, clearly saying, "*Azusa Street*: Pensacola, Florida. *Azusa Street*: Pensacola, Florida."

That day in January, 1989, I knew that God was going to send a revival to Pensacola, Florida. I realized even then that this revival would somehow touch the world just as the Azusa Street Revival in Los Angeles had changed the course of Church history in the early 1900's. From Pensacola, God would send laborers into the world who were full of the gifts of the Holy Spirit, and I knew God was calling me to go there.

I felt giddy with excitement at the thought of a worldwide revival, but more than that, I knew my call to Pensacola was serious and sure. I didn't know what my role would be, but I knew I had to go. I also felt sure that the revival would come through a ministry that I would somehow support and that humbling myself would be the key to my involvement. I just wondered where Pensacola was.

Responding to God's Call

As soon as I managed to get off the floor and regain my balance, I began searching for my travel group. They had been in a gift shop during the few short minutes I had been separated from them and God had revealed Himself to me. When I told these conservative Pentecostal ladies that God was going to send a worldwide revival to Pensacola, Florida, they just stared at me blankly. I got the impression that they thought I was cute to believe something so strongly. After I boarded the plane, I began to doubt the validity my revelation; but God again spoke to my spirit: "*Azusa Street*: Pensacola, Florida," and joy flooded my heart.

I was excited by the revelation God had given to me, but now I was even more disturbed by the growing suspicion that something about my life was terribly wrong. For some reason, I had agreed to travel to a Bible convention with people who were on the opposite pole from my doctrinal beliefs. The church I was involved in at that period of my life was a satellite extension of a church headquartered in California. I was beginning to realize that I had been trapped for years in this cultic, nondenominational group. They kept me and their other members bound by the pervasive teaching that God would not "keep us" and protect us from evil unless we followed that particular church's guidance. Although its teachers had painted a picture of all churches "outside" of our illuminated circle as being the "enemy," the little group of people I was traveling with were good people. They wanted nothing more than to give their all to God. (My old denomination kept many people entrapped for decades before it was finally shut down.)

I had just spent a weekend with people who served God with all that was in them, and they did it because they loved Him, not because they had to. They really didn't *fear* God in the "frightened" sense of the word, yet they served Him anyway. Although I felt they didn't have all their doctrines lined up with Scripture, I still saw they believed in the work of Christ's cross. Even more disturbing was the fact that these people had shown greater and more transparent love for me and for God than I had ever experienced. It was irritating. Somewhere inside me, I could almost hear a voice shouting, "Wake up! There are other people serving and loving God—even though they don't necessarily believe exactly like you do. You *need* them."

Worse than that, I began to see that my own involvement in separating others from the Body of Christ was rooted in a selfish spirit of control rather than in a "heart of mercy and concern" as I had pretended. What started out as simple error had grown into a destructive monster. I had become a part of the leadership of that denomination, and it was a shock to realize that I had imposed my fear of failure on others for selfish gain, notoriety, and numbers.

My days in that ministry were numbered from that point onward. God had opened my eyes, and I had no intention of going back into bondage. I had been set free to love God, to let others go free, and, in my own way, to finally "let God be God."

When I returned to my home in Marysville, Washington, just outside of Seattle, I immediately pulled out my U.S. map and looked for Pensacola. I had assumed it would be near Disney World in Orlando; however, I discovered it was much farther north, near the Alabama line. Within a few short months, I had sold all my belongings and moved to Pensacola. When I told my parents, friends, and neighbors I was moving 4,000 miles to a place I had never even seen because there was "going to be a revival there," most of them figured I had finally "gone off the deep end." In reality, I was simultaneously breaking from my past and pushing forward to what God had in store for me.

The Test of Obedience

I didn't realize it, but seven of the hardest years of my life lay ahead of me. When I got to Pensacola, I searched in church after church for revival, but it was nowhere to be found. There wasn't even a hint of it. To complicate things further, I was afraid of becoming caught up in bondage like I had just left. I had been controlled by man and had become a controller myself. Now I was too afraid of getting caught up in it again to settle in another church. As a result, when I failed to find "revival," I just kept moving from one church to another.

I even went to Brownsville Assembly of God for a while. I found the people to be kind and gentle, and I quickly came to respect Pastor Kilpatrick like no other man of God I had met before. The problem was that I brought my past baggage into the church with me, and since Brownsville hadn't yet experienced the arrival of revival, that bondage wasn't removed. In church after I church, I constantly found myself getting entangled in Bible knowledge competitions because of my argumentative, legalistic background. It seemed like every fellowship time led to another bout of "who knows more about the Bible," and I felt that prideful part of me rising up and being nurtured by the conflict. Time and time again, I moved on, driven by a deep fear of returning to what I had once been.

It was at that point, when I was discouraged, fearful, and without a church home, that heartrending strife and tragedy struck my home and brought disintegration. The pain and emotional strain of those days caused me to die in many ways. Almost four years had passed since my arrival in Pensacola, and I finally stopped looking for revival.

Lost in the Desert

I felt like life had "gone for the jugular vein." It was all I could do to get through each day. I was drowning in heartache, despair, and fear. I spent most of my time running from my fears. Again and again, I rehearsed in my mind just how hard my Christian life had been. I was completely oppressed, totally afraid, and utterly alone. For most of my adult life, I had been isolated by the walls of false doctrine that had been imposed and beaten into me. *How could I have been so foolish?!* The only consolation I had were the years I had spent on the floor before

God. At least those hours and days I spent crying before Him would be chalked up as "communion with God."

For more than a decade, I had given every minute and every bit of strength I had to a lie, and now in a puff of smoke, it was all gone. Worst of all, it had been a facade with layers of sin behind it all. Nearly a third of my life had been spent on something that now amounted to *nothing*. All that remained were my children and my desperate grip on the faint glimmer of hope that God was out there somewhere.

I tried to forget that I had once staunchly believed that a worldwide revival was coming to Pensacola. I avoided any acknowledgment that I had actually sold everything, uprooted my family, and left my West Coast heritage for a pilgrimage to the forbidden South. I had long since stopped believing that what I had heard so clearly and powerfully in that Wichita airport was from the Spirit of God. Every time these things managed to surface in my thoughts, I felt foolish.

I began to believe that it had been some delusion of my mind I had misinterpreted as the voice of God that had motivated me to move to the little Florida town of Pensacola near the Alabama border (otherwise known as "L.A." or "Little Alabama"). After several years of looking, waiting, and hoping, the batterings of life convinced me that my friends and family had been right all along: I had been crazy to leave Seattle to chase after some worldwide revival in a little Southern town I knew nothing about.

For the first three years after my move to Pensacola, my friend Paula would phone me from Seattle to ask, "Renee, did you ever find that revival you said would come to Pensacola?" For a long time my response was,

"Not yet." But in November, 1995, when she asked me about it for the last time, I nervously said, "No, and I don't want to talk about it. I must have really been 'out there' back then." I really didn't like talking to Paula or her daughter Jennifer because it brought back too many painful memories of the wasted years, errors, and deception. I couldn't understand why she and Jennifer still loved me, and I didn't want to talk about the revival that never came.

The Gentle Wooing of God's Spirit

Seven long years had passed since that day in the airport in Wichita. In January, 1996, I walked into the Brownsville revival for the first time, several weeks after I had first heard of it. I first heard about the revival at Brownsville Assembly of God when I tried to phone a friend and got her answering machine. Instead of the traditional "please leave a message" greeting, my friend's recorded voice announced that there was a powerful revival at Brownsville and that whoever was calling should be sure to attend.

At the time I felt convicted that I should go, but I quickly shrugged it off with the thought that it was just another run-of-the-mill revival excuse to get people into their church. Then I thought, *Boy, that girl has really gotten radical to put that announcement on her answering machine, of all places.*

Within a couple of weeks, another friend called and pointedly asked me to go to the revival with her. I was pretty scared by the prospect because I really did not think I was yet to the place where I could emotionally handle going to an actual revival. I also figured this would ultimately require the surrendering of my will back to God, and I wasn't sure I was ready to trust Him again.

God had nursed me back to a measure of wholeness after my escape from the West Coast and that stronghold of satanic fear. Even though I was a little better, I still felt like a shattered crystal glass that had been glued back together. I feared that even the slightest tremble or movement would shatter me again. I had suffered years of satanic attack through church hypocrisy and abuse, and it had all come to a head two years earlier. The result was so spiritually and emotionally devastating that I could barely function as a human being. God carefully and tenderly nursed me back into a relationship with Himself, like a nurse would carefully bring healing by gently and regularly changing the bandages on a wounded child.

I was afraid of being hurt by God because I had been hurt and deceived by man for so long. I could no longer read my Bible or get on my knees to pray. I was sure that God would reveal something that would be more than I could bear and I would somehow be pushed over the edge of my ability to cope. By His grace, God opened the door for me to work at a church preschool for several years. It was there, in an atmosphere designed to train children, that I saw God's love and unconditional acceptance revealed anew through His people.

Once a week, during preschool hours, we conducted a chapel service for the children. Hearing those simple Bible stories and singing children's praise songs again, took me back to the basics of seeing the purity of God's love. It wasn't easy. After I somehow managed to sit through the first chapel service, I was both surprised and relieved to realize I had made it through the 20-minute service without being hurt. It gave me a real sense of accomplishment.

After a few months of "children's therapy," I felt strong enough to sit in the back of the church for an adult Sunday service. Later, I was even able to move closer to the front.

Gradually I began to talk to God again while I walked around the house. Although I still couldn't read my Bible for about a year, I would cling to it in my sleep night after night. I can still remember the times throughout that summer that my friend Elaine read Scriptures to me over the phone for hours at a time.

A week or so after my friend's first invitation to go to the revival, I was "channel surfing" on the television when I stumbled across an interview with Pastor John Kilpatrick of Brownsville Assembly of God. Generally I didn't watch television during the afternoon, but during those lonely winter months, I often put my feet up and ate a sandwich while enjoying the "company" of some television personality explaining how to cook gourmet meals I knew I'd never make, or while admiring women who hauled huge pieces of plasterboard and got right in there with the men to nail the things up.

Thanks to the children's chapel services, I had reached a place where I could watch a few minutes of Christian television without turning away in pain and disgust. Every couple of nights, God's Spirit encouraged me to watch a Christian program for just a few more sentences or a few more minutes than I had the time before. I watched the last few minutes of the Kilpatrick interview, and I kept noticing how sweet and humble the pastor was as he encouraged viewers to go to the revival. Within minutes, I realized that I could go to this revival too, without any fear of being battered. There was also a very intense, "hyper" guy with blond hair named Steve

Hill being interviewed along with Pastor Kilpatrick. I didn't know quite what to think of him, but he adamantly agreed with the pastor that this revival in the Brownsville area of Pensacola was truly a phenomenal move of God.

I felt an old, familiar excitement rise up in me when I heard the men say the revival had been going on continuously for six months. They said a half-million people had already attended the services, coming from all over the world, and that 15,000 souls had been saved! I realized that this revival *might actually be the real thing.* I sensed God had somehow answered an unspoken prayer of my heart, and all I had to do was take a few more steps past my own fear.

As I watched the interview, it was glaringly evident that the life I had been building for myself had been on shifting sand in more ways than one. Hurricane Opal had left me in a state of isolation and introspection. The little place I had called my own on Pensacola Beach—along with half of everything I owned—had been ripped apart by the tidal surge. I even had to leave my job because the hurricane had left me in such a state of emotional shock; I knew I was unable to give my preschool class even one tenth of what they needed. When the interview was over, I turned off the television and sat in the middle of the living room floor. I thought about how tired I was. I was so very tired of fighting by myself.

First Taste of the Revival

The drive to the revival that first night felt a bit like a tooth extraction. I even amazed myself at how many reasons I gave for why my friend Elaine and I shouldn't be going. I was sure the people at the Brownsville Revival were going to be tight-lipped, self-righteous, condemning, cliquish, self-motivated, and just mean in general. Elaine and I both knew I was just rambling out of stress, so neither of us took anything I said seriously. It had been my idea for us to go; but when I mentioned that we might want to consider going real soon to this revival thing I'd heard about, Elaine took me by surprise and replied, "Well, why don't we go tomorrow night?" I resignedly just said, "Okay."

At first, I welcomed the usher's offer to help us find a seat. I fell in line behind Elaine as the older gentleman in a maroon jacket led the way down what seemed like the longest aisle I had ever seen. The more rows of church pews we passed as he led us closer and closer to the front of the sanctuary, the more I poked Elaine and laughingly chided her, "How close to the front is he going to take us anyway?" About halfway down, my cutting up turned to seriousness. I started to shake my head, telling Elaine and the usher, "Hey, this is close enough. We really don't want to sit *right* up front, ya know." This only seemed to make the usher walk faster.

About three-quarters of the way down the aisle I gave up. It appeared I did not have any choice in the matter. After what seemed like a ridiculously long walk, complete with the feeling that everyone in the place was looking at us, the usher pointed to our destination: third row from the front, directly under the speaker's podium. As I squeezed past the person sitting in the aisle seat of our designated row I jokingly commented, "I guess we *are* sitting 'right up front.'" Instead of recognizing my humor, his smile seemed to say, "Yeah, isn't it great." I thought, *I guess he doesn't get it.*

About the time we sat down, the music began to blare, and it was time to stand up. The lights were so bright I felt I needed sunglasses. I thought, *Boy, they must really want to be able to see each other.* I looked around to see what everyone was wearing to make sure I wasn't too off base wearing blue jeans, a casual shirt, and black army boots, especially since my plan for incognito observation of this "Brownsville Revival thing" from the back of the church certainly hadn't panned out.

I gradually got over the humor of being thrust into the hot seat and started to look around. All the people on the platform seemed nice enough. They didn't seem to be making it their business to judge me or make me feel uncomfortable. I didn't know the words to any of the songs, and I didn't pay any attention to them. The brilliance and heat of the lights, the high-voltage music, and the immediacy of being thrown right into the nerve center of the whole thing had me on sensory overload. Although it was a bit bizarre, it was certainly intriguing. Everybody seemed to be pretty happy about the whole thing.

This was definitely a "wait and see" deal that made me want to have my guard fully up and in place. I knew conviction of sin was right around the corner, and I needed to muster up all the self-protective shields of "I'm okay just the way I am" religiosity I could.

About two or three songs into the revival service that first night, I closed my eyes—partly to focus on God, partly to get away from the stress of those possible conviction bearers on the platform, and partly to appear righteous and adequately "churched." However, nothing around me appeared as I had expected. I had been in a lot of churches in my day (including Brownsville Assembly of God as it had been several years before), but what I was now witnessing wasn't church. It was more like an electric, color burst of lightning had struck and illuminated the whole place, and that illumination beamed through you from your insides out, making you feel warmly at home and strangely ill at ease, all at the same time.

Just when I started getting comfortable, the music stopped. When I opened my eyes, Pastor Kilpatrick was standing at the podium, which loomed a mere 15 feet away. I had always liked him, so I was glad to see him. Although he said only a few words, he sure said a lot.

He said, "There's a woman here who on her way here tonight went on and on with all kinds of reasons why she shouldn't be coming. Even though it was very hard for you to do, you came anyway. I need to tell you that you have allowed someone to take your joy away from you. God wants you to take it all off of you like a dirty old coat. He wants you to throw it to the ground and never, ever pick it up again in the name of Jesus."

I half felt like raising my hand and saying, "Yep, that's me," but I figured my bulging eyes gave me away anyway. For the rest of the service I kept visualizing myself throwing off that old coat. My hope began to rise as I considered the possibility of throwing off the fear, hopelessness, pain, and bondage that coat represented. The idea that it could be God's will for me to be free of condemnation and the yokes of man's curses gave me new hope for life. I was indeed like a drowning woman wearing an overcoat so heavy that it was dragging her down to death itself—until someone came along and said, "Hey, silly girl, take that coat off and put on this life jacket."

That next week before going back to the revival I pictured myself taking off that coat and all the bondages it represented. When I left my house to go back to the revival, I knew I was ready to trust God and to surrender my will back to Him.

Embracing the Revival of God

That second night Evangelist Steve Hill's message painted a real clear picture of the demonic forces behind the life I had already left behind in my heart. I had known it all before, but two years of Prozac and secular counseling fully armed me with the scapegoats of "poor me," "poor them," and "God would never judge or condemn 'poor us.'" I had a good old time listening as Steve exposed the devil and warned of the judgment of God without salvation through Jesus Christ. I was glad to be home.

When Steve gave the altar call, I turned to Elaine and told her I was going to the altar. She said, "But I thought we said we didn't need to do that because we believe in God and go to church and read the Bible and stuff." I replied, "All I know is, I've got to give my life back to God."

With a little extra encouragement from the song, "Run to the Mercy Seat," which was being powerfully sung by a young girl in the background, I just about knocked people over as I bolted past them out of that pew and down to the altar. When I got to the altar I said, "Jesus, I don't know how I'm going to do all that I need to do and get rid of all the stuff I need to get rid of. I'm just lining up behind You and trusting You to take me step by step and make it all possible because I sure can't do it on my own."

Steve was so excited at the number of people who had come to the altar that he told all of us to look around and see how many others had come forward. I looked to my right, and there on his knees was another good friend. When our eyes met, he smiled through the tears that were streaming down his face. His whole countenance was glowing. I knew he was at total peace for the first time in his life. It was the happiest day of my life as well. It was all I could do not to run over there and kneel down next to him, but I knew this was something I had to do on my own. I had to be able to look back on this moment and know that I had laid my life at the foot of the cross all by myself. I knew no one could save me or keep me but Jesus Christ. Somehow I knew I would be going this alone—just me and God.

I went back to my other church on Sunday morning because Steve said that they were not trying to take people from their churches, and that unless you knew you were called to Brownsville you needed to continue to support your home church and only come to Brownsville for revival. I also thought it was interesting that he and Pastor Kilpatrick said that they did not want anyone from another church to give their tithes to Brownsville because if they took a tithe that belonged to another church they would be cursed by God. They said they would only take offerings.

I desperately felt a need for spiritual food that Sunday morning. Valentine's Day was four days away, and I knew it was going to be a lonely one. I came out of my old church that Sunday morning so hungry for the Word of God that I cried on the way home. I thought I would die right there. All I had received was a sweet story to remind me to send my loved ones a Valentine's Day card. I was desperately afraid I would not make it through the temptations that lay ahead that week, and I dived into the

Bible when I got home. When God quickly fed my spirit-man, I knew I would be okay.

That Wednesday night Steve talked about the 17,500 souls who had been saved at the revival thus far. He described how a warlock had been delivered and was now serving Jesus and that a woman who had smoked pot for 15 years had been instantaneously set free at the altar and was serving God. He also said that pastors from around the country were coming to the revival, getting touched by God, and taking the anointing for revival back to their home churches. Then he suddenly and matter-of-factly stated: "This is a 1990's Azusa Street." The power of God hit my heart like a freight train. I was afraid to believe it was true. After all this time, God had been faithful to His promise He had made to me all those years ago. How could this be?

Ten months later, I wrote an article based on a sermon by Pastor Kilpatrick in which he describes how his heart goes out to those who have died in the desert. He concluded that powerful message by declaring that he has good news: "The river of God, the river of revival that contains the things of God that we have longed for and cried for, is once again flowing!"

Since that first week at the revival, I have personally seen tens of thousands of people come forward to be saved or to return to God. Not only have I experienced it myself, but every week I hear and see the amazing testimonies of people from all over the world who come to the Brownsville Revival and get saved, set free, healed, and filled with the Holy Spirit. As Sister Kilpatrick so beautifully puts it: "God is touching us, and we are touching the world!"

Chapter 3

"My House Shall Be Called the House of Prayer"

Nearly seven years had passed since I had last seen Jennifer in Seattle. Now here we were, standing together in the sanctuary of Brownsville Assembly of God Church in Pensacola, Florida. When she was only 12 years old, I had explained to her that I was leaving Washington state and moving away because there was going to be a worldwide revival in Pensacola, Florida. Now, after so long and so much, we were finally here. It didn't seem possible. We held hands and extended them toward Heaven and sang at the top of our lungs with 3,000 other worshipers, "This is the year of the favor of the Lord!" Indeed it was! Indeed it is!

The reality of the revival was more powerful than I had ever dreamed possible. Having Jennifer there beside me was simply an added statement of victory. Each word of the song illustrated, punctuated, and strengthened my faith. I was determined to do whatever I had been called to do all those years ago. As I held Jennifer's hand there were no tears, only determination, as we sang:

The Spirit of the sovereign Lord is upon you
Because He has anointed you
To preach good news
The Spirit of the sovereign Lord is upon you
Because He has anointed you
To preach good news

He has sent you to the poor
(This is the year)
To bind up the brokenhearted
(This is the day)
To bring freedom to the captives
(This is the year)
To release the ones in darkness.

This is the year
Of the favor of the Lord.
This is the day
Of the vengeance of our God
This is the year
Of the favor of the Lord.
This is the day
Of the vengeance of our God

The Spirit of the sovereign Lord is upon you
Because He has anointed you
To preach good news
The Spirit of the sovereign Lord is upon you
Because He has anointed you
To preach good news

He will comfort all who mourn
(This is the year)
He will provide for those who grieve in Zion
(This is the day)
He's pouring out His oil of gladness
(This is the year)
Instead of mourning we will praise...[1]

I had been beaten down and beaten up, but even when I had stopped believing, God was still working on my behalf. He restored my faith and set me free. My God was truly an awesome God. He had moved earth, Heaven above, and hell below for me.

I had lost contact with her mother, so I had written a short note to Jennifer: "Tell your mother I have found the revival. Souls are being saved by the thousands. The power of God is so strong that you feel you can almost cut the thickness of the glory cloud with a knife. Come down as soon as you can!"

Jennifer could only stay in Pensacola for a few days because she had just completed U.S. Army boot camp and needed to report for duty soon. We decided to see if we could talk to Pastor Kilpatrick during the break in the service before the message that night. We went up on the steps of the platform and quietly waited while he spoke briefly with a few ministers who seemed anxious to talk with him. I knew confirmation of my testimony was important, so we waited our turn. Pastor Kilpatrick turned to us, and as he sat down in his chair he nodded toward Jennifer and lightheartedly asked, "Now who do we have here?" By this simple act he made me feel that we had his undivided attention. I appreciated that. I really hadn't tried to talk with him or Steve Hill before that night because it seemed there were so many others who needed their attention.

I was delighted by Jennifer's eagerness and sense of urgency when she said, "Pastor Kilpatrick, we have something very important to tell you." After she looked over at me she continued, "Seven years ago, when I was just a little girl still living in Seattle, Renee told me there was going to be a major revival in Pensacola—and now were here!"

Pastor Kilpatrick asked if we knew about Dr. David Yonggi Cho's prophecy given five and a half years before the revival hit, and when we said we hadn't, he remarked, "I guess you got it before him then." We all counted up the years and realized it was true. Then Jennifer told Pastor Kilpatrick that she would be on her way to Korea that next week. He was obviously surprised by the apparent coincidence between Dr. Cho's homeland and Jennifer's destination. Jennifer suddenly realized that she had forgotten to tell him she was in the Army. She quickly explained that her next duty station was Korea, and he asked if she would be going to one of Dr. Cho's churches while she was stationed there. She nodded and said she planned to now—a lot of people at the revival that night had urged her to go once they heard she was on her way to Korea. Jennifer beamed when Pastor Kilpatrick asked her to be sure and tell Dr. Cho that "John Kilpatrick said hello."

Pastor Kilpatrick often illustrates the sovereignty of what God is doing at Brownsville by telling the thousands of first-time visitors who come to the revival each week about Dr. Cho's detailed prophecy five years before the revival began.

In the Foreword of Pastor Kilpatrick's book, *Feast of Fire*, Dr. Cho described his prophecy:

"America has always been close to my heart. Thousands of American soldiers fought in the Korean War, many giving their lives so my country could be free. That is why I pray daily for America. That is why I lead my congregation of 700,000 to pray for America in our twelve weekly worship services.

"When I was ministering in Seattle, Washington, in 1991, I became deeply concerned about the spiritual decline in America. I began to pray even more earnestly for revival in these United States. As I prayed, I felt the Lord prompt me to get a map of America, and to point my finger on the map. I found myself pointing to the city of Pensacola in the Florida panhandle.

"Then I sensed the Lord say, 'I am going to send revival to the seaside city of Pensacola, and it will spread like a fire until all of America has been consumed by it.'

"That revival fire has now come to Pensacola's Brownsville Assembly of God church."[2]

Brownsville Assembly of God completed its new church building in 1991, the same year Dr. Cho gave his prophecy. I attended one of the first services in the new building, and the sanctuary seemed so huge that I wondered if they would ever be able to fill the auditorium with people. No one was sitting in the balcony or in any of the pews in the side sections. There just seemed to be way too much space, especially after the congregation's years of being crunched together so tightly in the former building (now referred to as "the chapel"). At first I really wondered if the church had bitten off more than it could chew, and I hoped they didn't end up looking silly because they could never fill the place. Then Pastor Kilpatrick came out and started preaching. I realized it didn't matter whether they filled up the building or not; that church was definitely hearing the Word of God preached in power. (I often regret not staying at Brownsville from the start, but my fear, and later my shame, were too great at that time.)

Years later, on the weekend Brownsville Assembly passed its one-year anniversary of continuous revival, I chuckled at my doubt about the new sanctuary ever filling up. I saw thousands of people eagerly run into the building from every available door, filling the sanctuary within three minutes. I laughed about my early doubts and mused, "This is one of those 'Look what the Lord has done!' moments."

Prayer Preparation

I am fascinated when I consider how many elements of old-fashioned obedience and miraculous preparation went into the revival. Pastor Kilpatrick often emphasizes that prayer is the primary catalyst for revival. Many times, I've heard him admit that two and a half years before the beginning of the revival, it had been very hard for him to step out in faith to institute congregational prayer meetings on Sunday nights instead of the traditional preaching and teaching format. He said he had been severely attacked by a gripping fear that people would stop coming on Sunday nights, but God reminded him of the Scripture, "My house shall be called the house of prayer" from Matthew 21:13. That left him with only one choice: to obey God's mandate.

In his book, *Feast of Fire*, Pastor Kilpatrick wrote: "I started to see that if I took a pie gauge of everything that was being done in our church and broke that pie up, prayer was usually the thinnest slice. The biggest slice of the pie were the preaching, the worship, the offering, and a little bit of altar time when we prayed with people. The

Holy Spirit showed me that though His house was supposed to be a house of prayer, ours was really everything but prayer. Something had to change."[3]

Pastor Kilpatrick obeyed God's direction, and when Sunday night prayer meetings were initially instituted at Brownsville in August of 1992, attendance began to increase rather than decrease. Twelve beautifully tapestried banners were created in response to instructions Pastor Kilpatrick received from God. He wanted to divide the church auditorium into segments and to use banners for each prayer category to help people stay focused in prayer. Despite Pastor Kilpatrick's fear that the people would stop coming, Sunday night attendance soon grew by over 20 percent.

The church continued the Sunday night prayer meetings for three years. About six months into the revival, the pastor changed the prayer meetings from Sunday nights to Tuesday. Those Tuesday night prayer meetings have provided some of my greatest times of empowerment in Holy Ghost power and strength. It has been in those meetings on my knees that God built my faith in Him as a loving Father. Through these times I've learned to declare: "I am going to pray as much and as authoritatively as it takes, and nothing is going to mess with my church, my family, or me."

The Key to Continued Revival

Tuesday night is the most important night of the week at the Brownsville Revival, and it became the most important night in my week as well. It is the night that 1,000 or more prayer warriors gather to pray for that week's revival services. Brother Dick Reuben, a Messianic Jew who regularly ministers at Brownsville, often leads the prayer service. He often says, "As the Tuesday night prayer meeting goes, so goes the revival for the week." It isn't at all unusual for us to hear visitors who have come for a full week of revival services tell us that the Tuesday prayer meeting was the most powerful night of that week!

During these times of intense intercessory prayer, the darkness is broken up in the heavenlies, and we drive away any spiritual oppression that may have been left behind from the many deliverances that took place the week before. This is also the time when we all gather together in the name of Jesus, in one spirit and one accord, to contend in prayer and ask God to send forth His Spirit to the far corners of the earth to bring in His harvest of souls. By the name and blood of Jesus Christ, the powers of darkness are commanded to release their hold on souls that are called into God's Kingdom. Incredible power is released when 1,000 faces and hearts bow before the Almighty God to humbly ask Him to open the heavens so that His gifts may flow freely for His glory and honor alone.

Often those who come to Tuesday night prayer meeting for the first time do not know what to expect. When you first enter the sanctuary you sense that it is "charged" with a surety that something mighty is about to happen. This is warfare. Day-to-day and personal concerns quickly fall to the wayside because it soon becomes apparent that there is a greater job to do, a task of utmost significance and gravity. The first 15 minutes or so are usually devoted to personal meditation and prayer, when we all move to a place of complete focus on God.

Worship music plays softly in the background as we all turn our thoughts and meditations upward and inward toward God's indwelling Spirit. Hundreds of guests who have come from all over the world intermingle with prayer warriors who have been there regularly. No one cares about our differences of background or theology because we all serve the same Master. By the time the meeting starts, the prayer coordinator has already welcomed all the visitors and told them a little bit about the general format and purpose of the meeting, but even the visitors instinctively know that the true leader of the meeting is the Holy Ghost.

During those first few minutes of personal meditation, the spirit of repentance falls powerfully over those who are gathered together before the Father's throne. God's awesome presence is unmistakable. The magnificence of His presence sets everyone's priorities in order very quickly. God has business to do and those who have chosen to be a part of this night's battle soon realize that they are there to do what it takes to get that business done.

The call to repentance from sin and selfishness is imperative because God wants to remove all hindrances to His work. Kneeling at the altar or between the pews, those who came in as individuals become unified by the corporate purpose, the purpose of putting on the mind of Christ to glorify God and do His work. The battle begins with teams of two to five individuals locking arms to drive out demons that may be lingering from the week before. With arms locked, hundreds of teams march through each room of the campus, the balcony, the restrooms, and choir loft.

In the power of the Holy Ghost and in the blood and name of Jesus Christ, spiritual darkness is driven out when it is rebuked and commanded to go. Through speaking in tongues and petitioning God, His anointing is released. Corporate spiritual warfare brings the spiritual environment into order. Faith is built and strengthened with each marched step. God's army is out to defeat and cast out darkness, and God's people will settle for nothing short of total victory. Our days of being harassed, discouraged, or hindered by satan and his imps are over.

God's people are taking charge through the power of the Holy Ghost. Anything that would exalt itself against the knowledge of God is cast down and cast out to the outer dry places of the earth.[4] Anything that would try to cause distraction from the hearing of God's words of life and truth is commanded to leave. Anything that would exalt itself against the leadership of the church and cause division or accusation is driven out by the name and blood of Jesus Christ. Pride, wrath, division, jealousy, doubt, affliction, confusion, perversion, distortion, rebellion, and sorcery are rebuked and brought down.

In the nursery area, families and workers are prayed for, and spirits of accident and infirmity are bound. Hands are laid on the doors of church leaders' offices. Spiritual hindrances are commanded to keep their hands off of them, and God is petitioned to place mighty angels of protection round about them. As teams pass one another in the hall, no one stops to personally acknowledge one another because each team is at war and cannot allow distractions from the singleness of its purpose.

After the spiritual environment has been "swept and cleaned," it is time to ask God to move in lives, families, ministries, and lands. The 10 to 12 prayer banners posted at various stations around the sanctuary help to guide those who are praying. These beautifully stitched tapestries suggest the categories of healing, families, pastors, ministries, spiritual warfare, Jerusalem, revival, souls, catastrophes, children, schools, our country, and our Bridegroom's return for His Bride, the Church.

The intercessors are clearly instructed that the banners only suggest ideas of things to pray for and are not for any other purpose. They help individuals to stay focused in prayer and avoid distraction. Those stationed at the individual category areas usually petition God individually. Someone at the family banner may pray for his or her own family, another may pray for God to bless the families who will be coming to the revival that week, and still others may pray for families within their church or community.

Intercessory tears may flow freely at one banner while spiritual warfare is waged at another. Thousands of prayers are lifted up into the heavenlies in each passing minute. The presence and glory of the Lord ministers to all and brings confident faith and hope in Him whose ears are open to each petition.

Some may only move to two or three banners during this time, focusing on the categories that are their deepest concern at that time. Others may move quickly, spending only a few minutes in each category as they feel led to take on the burden or petition of each area.

During this time of individual prayer, the corporate element remains strong because the group's faith is being built up together. Those gathered around one banner regularly begin to agree with one another in prayer as they lift up their burdens to God. When breakthrough in prayer is felt, each will move on to his or her individual prayer burdens.

Waging War for Lost Souls

Many tears are shed at the banner representing the "souls" category. Here the battle is waged for the salvation and deliverance of loved ones. Intercessors cry and contend for the souls of a lost and dying world. Scrolled bits of pieces of paper bearing the names of loved ones are piled up at the bottom of the banner. They are then gathered up and taken to the leaders of prayer teams who will pray for them throughout the week. Names and pictures of loved ones have also been left on a table for anointed prayer. Many testimonies of salvation, healing, deliverance, and answers to prayer have been born out of pictures, personal belongings, and prayer request cards laid there in faith and prayed over by the church leadership.

The intercessors are then asked to gather at the altar area to call for souls from the far corners of the earth to be brought out of darkness and into the marvelous light of Jesus—from the east, west, north, and south. The spiritual warfare and souls banners are posted at the south end of the building. Prayer warriors stand unified in spiritual battle array with their hands stretched forth in power. Souls are called out from cities, countries, and continents to the south. Powers of spiritual wickedness in high places are commanded to release their holds on individuals and communities by the blood and name of Jesus Christ. Corporate prayer calls upon God to send forth His mighty anointing and bring in the harvest of souls. A prayer captain on the platform, with microphone in hand, steadfastly leads the charge of prayer; and with a mighty roar, God's army is sent forth in each direction, first to the south, then the west, east, and north.

The first time this charge went out from Brownsville Assembly of God a year and a half ago, several individuals were sitting on the steps of the church the next morning when an usher came to open the church doors. The usher asked the young people, "Is there something I can do to help you?" They responded, "We're here to get saved." At the time of this writing, over 100,000 people have come to the altar and received Jesus Christ as their personal Lord and Savior.

After the spiritual charge that wars for the lost, the faces and attention of each person are then focused upward as humble hearts ask God for an open heaven through the coming week of revival: "It is only by Your blessed mercy and grace that there is ever even one more moment of the glory of Your awesome manifested presence that transforms lives and hearts. We, with so many others, are desperate for a touch from You, God. Thank You for all You have done, even this very night. We are not worthy, Lord, but for some reason You have chosen to visit Your people one more time. Lord, continue to have mercy on the lost and hurting. Have mercy on our land, on the nations of the world, and on us. All glory and honor belongs to You."

In each revival prayer meeting, I "war in prayer" and worship God with thousands of people from Brownsville and from all over the world. The prayer banners have actually helped me to keep my focus, and they remind me of particular prayer needs. The fruits of those prayer meetings dispersed the pastor's original fears and have surpassed everyone's wildest dreams. God knew all along that hundreds of thousands of believers would hear about the prayer meetings at the Brownsville Revival. They have been destined to come from the far corners of the earth to pray and to be prayed for, and to receive an anointing for prayer that they can take back to others in their towns, cities, and homelands.

Personal Preparation

I have heard Pastor Kilpatrick describe several areas in which God required him to change or step out in faith before revival would come. My heart breaks every time I hear him tell of the day God spoke to him while he was driving down the road: "If you don't get rid of that critical spirit, I am going to pass you by." Pastor Kilpatrick immediately pulled the car over to the side of the road, put his head on the steering wheel, and repented.

Another time in early 1995, Pastor Kilpatrick was watching Benny Hinn minister on television. Brother Hinn prophesied that in March God would begin the process of bringing revival to the United States and that by June God would have found the place where He would pour out His Spirit. Pastor Kilpatrick says he crawled over to the television on his hands and knees and placed his hand on the screen. Then he prayed, "God, if You are really going to send revival someplace in the United States, please let that someplace be Brownsville. God, please don't pass us by." God heard that prayer. On Father's Day of that year (1995), the river of revival and the powerful presence of God rushed into the sanctuary at Brownsville Assembly of God. Pastor Kilpatrick was still grieving over the recent loss of his mother, so he had asked his longtime friend, Evangelist Steve Hill, to preach the morning and evening services that day. Steve shifted back and forth, bounced up and down, and wrung his hands throughout his message. He declared over and over, "Folks, God is going to move this morning. God is going to move this morning!"

Brother Hill was right. When he gave the altar call, 1,000 people flooded the altar for salvation and other prayer requests. Pastor Kilpatrick says, "I looked out in the congregation and it seemed like grenades were detonating around the building as people first in one area and then another suddenly fell to the ground or to their knees under the power of God." He explains that when the spiritual river rushed into the sanctuary, it sounded like a train or a mighty wind. This conservative pastor says his ankles suddenly "flipped over sideways," and he could no longer stand up on the stage. That powerful flow of the river of God brought refreshing, life, anointing, healing, unity, holiness, and new depths of intimacy with God. It was to touch hundreds of thousands in the weeks, months, and years to come.

Many of the people in that momentous Father's Day service never did make it to lunch with their natural fathers. Many stayed in the glorious presence of their heavenly Father throughout most of the day and returned again that night. Ever since that first day, Pastor Kilpatrick, Evangelist Hill, and others have prayed, "God, just one more night. Just bless us one more night with Your wonderful presence." And night after night, month after month, God has graciously, mercifully, and awesomely done just that.

God's Team Preparation

I often hear other pastors comment about the obvious respect that Pastor Kilpatrick and Steve Hill have for one another. They remark on how unique it is that the revival doesn't revolve around just one man and that everyone remains so humble. I've noticed that Lindell Cooley, the worship director, humbly flows with the ministry team when the direction of the song service is suddenly interrupted by prophecy, prayer, or song requests from the platform. Lindell has commented that these interruptions or changes in direction were once hard for him, but God has humbled him in that area. I believe God has worked through that humility and anointed Lindell to pave the way for the move of His Spirit in each service.

Pastor Kilpatrick and Steve Hill may outwardly appear to be the "odd couple" of ministry, but the fruits of their "tag team" ministry are dynamic. Tony Taylor, who was saved at Brownsville a year before the revival, said in an interview that "the dynamics of the odd couple" had set him free from condemnation. Tony was once a nightclub bouncer and bartender, and even though everyone at Brownsville loved and received him after he was saved, the devil kept beating him down with the thought that he had sinned too much. Tony has described how the Lord led him to victory over condemnation, "But then I later saw how Pastor, with all his stature and dignity, shared his pulpit with Steve Hill, an ex-drug addict. I was freed up after that."

Steve Hill was radically saved from a life of crime and chronic drug addiction in the 1970's. He received training from several mighty men of God, including the late Leonard Ravenhill. He went on to become an Assemblies of God evangelist. He helped plant churches for seven years during the great Argentine revival. Then he ministered in South America, Russia, and around the United States for three years before the beginning of the Brownsville Revival. He has been instrumental in establishing churches and drug rehabilitation centers in several areas of the world. (Pastor John Kilpatrick, on the other hand, heard the call of God on his life in junior high school and began pastoring his first church at the ripe old age of 20!)

Lindell Cooley transformed the original odd couple into the "odd trio." Raised in a Pentecostal home by parents who ministered musically to both white and black churches, Lindell toured the country in his youth as the pianist for the late Rusty Goodman. Later, he landed in Nashville, Tennessee. There he earned national recognition as a record producer, studio musician, and worship leader—but God had yet another plan in mind for Lindell. Somehow Pastor Kilpatrick got this dynamic young man to move from his seat of success in the Nashville scene to sleepy Pensacola, Florida—*before the revival began.* When I first began attending the revival, Lindell's hair reached almost to his shoulders. Then he returned from a visit to Israel with a radical goatee and mustache. A few months later, he began to arrive with a clean-shaven face. Finally, he emerged with a preppy, short-hair look. These details only further demonstrate the magnificence of God's sovereign ways that have brought these three very different men together to serve Him in unity.

To the natural mind, the team of "Pastor Watchful"; "Evangelist Street Smart"; and "Music Director Trendy" is inconceivable. But spiritual hunger, righteous humility, love for souls, and the grace of God combine to allow the river of revival to flow in unity with the Spirit of God under the leadership of these men. To His own glory, God chose a team of "no-names." He anointed men who had no fame or significant national acclaim to lead His revival. God chose vessels who would "let God be God."

I believe there is even more to it than that. I believe God chose Brownsville Assembly of God because its people loved the Word of God. They also loved their pastor because he preached God's Word without compromise and refused to tolerate sin. The Lord chose to visit a church that welcomed newcomers with open arms and for many years faithfully sought His face for holiness and revival. Perhaps this is because over and over again, Pastor Kilpatrick warns his congregation: "We must be ever so cautious to never take what God is doing for granted." The congregation continues to gratefully praise God for His river of life and respond in obedience to Him. God has continued to pour out His anointing upon Brownsville, and He receives all of the glory.

Endnotes

1. Excerpt from "Spirit of the Sovereign God," Andy Park, Copyright © 1994, Mercy/Vineyard Publishing (adm. by Music Services)/ASCAP. Reproduced by permission.

2. John Kilpatrick, *Feast of Fire* (Pensacola, FL: self-published by John Kilpatrick, 1995), vii.

3. Kilpatrick, *Feast of Fire*, 42-43.

4. See Second Corinthians 10:4-5 and Matthew 12:43.

Chapter 4

The River Is Here

Once I got a taste of true revival during the winter of 1996, I just couldn't stay away. Everything the world of sin and dead religion had to offer just seemed utterly wasteful and increasingly ridiculous. I couldn't help but tell other people about the Brownsville Revival. (I still can't help it—the news is too good to keep to myself.) I always hope they will listen and seize the opportunity to go check out the revival for themselves. I find it hard to be laid back or casual about the revival, and I usually describe it in my own enthusiastic way, saying something like, "You've absolutely got to go! The music will blow your socks off, and the presence of God is so strong that it totally boggles your mind! Sometimes it's so powerful you can barely stand up."

In the months that followed that first exposure to God's *shekinah* presence, I experienced the glory of God in greater and greater degrees. It was like experiencing a little bit of Heaven each time we gathered together in His presence. My heart soared with hope and melted in His holiness. I was set free on the wings of His praises, and I was broken in the presence of the Mighty One. I, who was weak, became strong in the strength of the Conqueror. I was unified with others in His love, and I was brought low in the worship of my Almighty Creator and Master.

After my very first revival service, I always sat right up front. Even though I still felt very intimidated by everything and everyone on the platform, I consistently "took the bull by the horns" each night I attended the revival. Right or wrong, I figured that the power was probably strongest up front, so I thought, *Why not get the most out of it?* By the spring of 1996, my favorite area—three rows from the front and to the far right of the podium (where Pastor Kilpatrick and Steve Hill can't see you until they get up to speak)—was converted into a reserved seating area for visiting pastors and their wives. But until that time, I considered it mine.

Some people will tell you they have a favorite part of the revival service, but I've always felt that each part is important in its own right. At first, I attended the revival services just to help me stay strong enough to resist temptation and depression each week. I had come to the revival in serious need of healing, restoration, and refreshing, and I had been under medication for depression and stress for some time. Nevertheless, the effect of God's presence was so strong that I was able almost immediately to safely cut my Prozac dose down to less than half. (I knew that I wasn't ready to take the plunge and quit "cold turkey" yet. Every time over the past two years I had tried to take that step I had ended up in the doctor's office in tears as a total "basket case.")

"More, Lord"

For the first few weeks, I only attended one service a week, but as I began to feel a greater urgency for holiness in my life I increased my attendance. The revival may well be the only "addiction" that is truly healthy for me. I found the more I received from God, the more I wanted Him. In fact, that was one of the keynote revival phrases: "More, Lord." I really didn't have a clue about what "More, Lord" meant, but I knew that I was becoming more and more hungry for what God wanted to give me. I also knew that He was the only one who knew what I needed each moment, and in the hours, weeks, and years to come. Night after night I quietly asked for "more." And night after night God's answer was, "Yes." He gave me far and above what I could possibly conceive or ask for. The greatest things I received during those early weeks were peace, hope for the future, and a firm faith that God would keep me victorious over sin.

I quickly discovered that every time I entered His presence, any darkness that was trying to catch up with me was scattered. My faith rose higher and higher. I witnessed with boldness and felt the Holy Spirit flow freely through the congregation offering salvation, deliverance, healing, encouragement, purpose, and love to those who were gathered in His name.

Most services began when Lindell Cooley hit the first note on his keyboard to begin worship. At that moment everyone rose to their feet. Sometimes I had the sensation that we were all aboard a big airplane that had just taken off. In those early services, I watched the mouths of the praise team leaders on stage closely to figure out what they were singing. I became pretty good at lip reading, but I could not remember the words on my own for months. One thing was certain: I felt the jubilation and rejoiced in the praise to God. I must admit that it felt good to express such happiness in a church service. It was also fun.

In every service, I tried to focus my mind on God throughout the worship. Worship really didn't come to me naturally, but I gave it my best shot because I desperately wanted to honor Him. Later, I understood the "why" of it when Lindell explained that *anyone* can praise God, but that someone really has to *know* Him to worship Him. He illustrated his point with a Scripture: "The mountains and the hills shall break forth before You into singing, and all the trees of the field shall clap their hands."[1] Several months later, the Spirit of God moved upon my body while we praised and worshiped Him and bent me over like a young sapling. In the beginning, however, I was like a slightly stiffer tree in the field happily clapping along to the music.

At first, I was really only trusting God "by the skin of my teeth." I felt as though fear was still under my skin waiting to jump out and say, "See, I've got ya!" However, I kept doing what I knew to do, which was to let God get rid of more and more of the vain philosophies and destructive habits I had picked up during my "vacation in hell." I just kept praying and going to the revival to soak in God's presence.

Almost without fail, every revival service for months featured the song, "We Will Ride." When the praise team would begin to sing those familiar words, some of us would begin to grin at one another in joy and amusement; yet my faith rose higher each time I visualized us riding on white horses behind the Lord Jesus Christ. From the very first service, that song verbalized our personal and corporate commitment to go wherever, do whatever, and be whomever the Lord required. The first time I heard it, I said, "That's my favorite song." I think I felt more unity with the rest of the church family as we sang that song than at any other time. Perhaps this was because it is based on one of the most vivid passages in the Book of Revelation:

And I saw heaven opened, and behold a white horse; and He that sat upon him was called Faithful and True, and in righteousness He doth judge and make war. His eyes were as a flame of fire, and on His head were many crowns; and He had a name written, that no man knew, but He Himself. And He was clothed with a vesture dipped in blood: and His name is called The Word of God. And the armies which were in heaven followed Him upon white horses, clothed in fine linen, white and clean (Revelation 19:11-14).

Finally, after about six months, my 13-year-old daughter Rachel said that she just couldn't take much more of that song. God must have heard her because we stopped singing it so often shortly after that.

Signs of God's Renewing

I quickly discovered that Pastor John Kilpatrick wasn't the only one God was asking to change during the revival. Sometimes I saw an older lady, her hair pinned up in a Pentecostal bun, waltz right around the front of the church at the altar area during the praise and worship time. The first time I saw it, I blinked a couple of times because I thought I was seeing things. Then I asked my friend next to me, "Do you see that? I wouldn't be caught dead ever doing something like that." I forgot that God was listening. Boy, was I in for a surprise!

After a few songs, "Dad" (oh, I mean Pastor Kilpatrick) would come out and welcome everyone to the revival. The rich atmosphere of love and belonging made me feel like we had all come there for Sunday dinner. I have always appreciated the loving way he does that. Pastor Kilpatrick frequently gives a word from the Lord for an individual or for the whole church. I know that Pastor Kilpatrick's prophetic word for me my first night at the revival certainly marked a turning point in my life. I love to hear these messages, and I know they are definitely from the Lord. Some people have joked that they were once afraid to hang around Pastor Kilpatrick because they felt like he could read their mind, and I think everyone just really wants to please him because he carries such a mantle of authority. In truth, Pastor Kilpatrick has always wanted what is best for everybody, and if God gives him discernment on an issue, it is because it is something we need to hear.

Discernment has played an important role throughout Pastor Kilpatrick's pastoral ministry. He once told us about an evangelist who spoke at Brownsville Assembly before the revival came. Pastor Kilpatrick said that he felt so uncomfortable about the man's message and ministry that he paid him out of his own pocket and sent him on his way rather than risk the curse of paying him out of church funds. That very night, God gave Pastor Kilpatrick a vision of the man in a bar in Alabama doing things that the pastor wouldn't repeat. Shortly after that, Pastor Kilpatrick called the man and told him what he had seen in the vision. The man burst into tears. The devil had assured that minister, "You're out of town. No one will ever know if you sin tonight." He had forgotten that God sees all, and that He often reveals it to His people. God once gave me a vision of a man in a pornography shop. When I approached that individual about it, he admitted his sin as well. God definitely moves in words of knowledge, and it is a gift that is sorely needed in the Church today.

Evangelist Steve Hill also gives words of knowledge on a regular basis. Most of these are addressed to individuals during the revival altar calls. Time and time again, he has been right on track. One time a barroom bouncer was sitting up in the balcony when Steve Hill looked up to where he was sitting. He pointed his finger at the man and said, "God knows about your drug problem." That was a definite "Whoa!" experience for the young man. He obeyed the Spirit of God and went to the altar. That night he was instantaneously delivered of his drug problem and has testified many times to God's transforming power.

Another time, a large number of people had already gone down to the altar, but Steve was still encouraging people to come down for salvation. Suddenly, he abruptly stated there was a man wearing white tennis shoes and blue jeans who still needed to come down. Of course, when I looked up, I saw a man with white tennis shoes and blue jeans headed for the altar, and the place exploded with applause and joy at the man's obedience. I thought, *Boy, that Hill guy sure is brave.* Incidentally, the man in white tennis shoes and his wife became friends of mine later on. He explained to me that God had been pulling on his heart, urging him to go, but when Steve called him out, he knew he had to obey. After that he had enough joy in the Lord for any ten men!

Steve Hill usually ministers after the "break" in the Brownsville Revival service. Early on, Pastor Kilpatrick and Brother Hill realized the limitations of the human body and attention span. They also knew that the Holy Spirit was well able to negotiate a ten-minute break in the middle of a three-hour service, so they instituted an intermission at mid service. I enjoyed the time to talk to people, but this time also offered the Holy Spirit a tremendous opportunity to work on my insecurities and secret prejudices. I had never liked to talk to anyone I didn't already know. Frankly, in my early days at the revival, I was still pretty arrogant. In my opinion at the time, most of the people in those services were too "square-looking" for me. To me that meant they were "holy-rollers with condemning attitudes." I consciously steered clear of such people and actually pretended I didn't see them.

I was so self-righteous in my determination to never be a "Pentecostal separatist" that I told one lady I would never stop wearing blue jeans and casual clothing to church, "Because as soon as you start putting on the Pentecostal garb no one will ever take you seriously when you witness to them." At the same time, I totally missed the fact that the lady I was talking to was dressed in "Pentecostal garb"! Of course, God saw to it that I was soon knocked off of my high horse so I could learn the value of seeking moderation in all things. Looking back, I realize now that when I saw that dear sister, I flashed back to the pictures I had of myself from the period I was depressed and downtrodden by the religious cult on the West Coast. In those days I always dressed in drab and conservative clothing. My oldest daughter called it my "I have no life" era.

The Holy Spirit immediately convicted me of my "reverse snobbishness," but I wondered if it was too late. I repented to God, thanked Him for the lesson on the spot, and told Him I believed I had learned a major lesson about not hurting others while promoting my personal bandwagon. I also halfway suspected I'd be dressing a little differently in the near future.

After the break in each revival service, an offering is usually received. One of the most common criticisms offered by people who have never attended the revival themselves is that Brownsville Assembly is only after the tithes of all the neighboring churches. I love to tell people how Pastor Kilpatrick (or one of the elders) always explains that they don't want anyone in the service to put their tithes in the offering plate. Anyone from another church should only give a freewill offering. In other words, everyone should give the ten percent tithe of their income to their home church, not to Brownsville Assembly of God. Pastor Kilpatrick has always been adamant about this because he feels so strongly about planting the tithe in the local storehouse. If any visitor wants to give an offering over and above the tithe given to his or her local church, that person is welcome to do so. Of course in my early days, I wasn't giving anything to either. That too was about to change.

Response to Revival

Steve Hill's evangelistic messages during the evening revival services were both entertaining and convicting. He definitely made me laugh, but at the same time his messages made me want to repent. In those early days every time he looked at me I felt like he was challenging me to get down to the altar because he was sure I had sin in my life. Later on, I realized that I was still dealing with a spirit of self-condemnation stemming from years of bondage preaching. This understanding didn't come until I was totally delivered from that spirit sometime later.

But for those first few months, I thought I'd be worn completely out by the time he finished preaching each night.

Nevertheless, I dearly loved and respected Steve Hill. I was absolutely confident that if I brought friends into the revival service, they would never leave the same way they came in. I had brought friends to other churches in the past, and afterward they had just gone on their merry way. I remember once going to church with my friend Elaine and leaving with a sense of intense disappointment because I knew we were still in the same mess we were in before going. Oh sure, we left feeling a little "mushy" about God and mankind, but we were still in the same old pit.

In spite of the powerful ministry of the revival, however, God still leaves the burden of responsibility with the individuals. Some of my friends came to the revival a few times and were really touched by God, but because they tried to serve God "just a little" while also holding on to their old lifestyle, they eventually slid away (and broke my heart in the process). One friend told me that if I ever got her into church, she'd never leave. Well, I got her into church, but when the conviction of the Holy Spirit hit, I thought she was going to take my head off during the altar call! We were sitting up front, as usual, when Steve Hill started to ask people to come forward for salvation. My friend suddenly started looking around for her daughter and saying in loud tones that she needed to leave because the service was running too late. Everyone around us was sitting quietly, and a lot of people were looking our direction. Then Brother Hill told everyone to stand up and ask the person next to them if they needed forgiveness. I sheepishly asked my friend if she needed forgiveness and she began to rant and rave to me about how she already went to church and didn't need anybody trying to get her to the altar. (We both knew better.)

The following morning during a heated phone conversation, my friend hurled accusations at me about Steve Hill and Brownsville Assembly that struck like daggers into the core of my heart. I was so grieved and hurt by her words that I could barely breathe. I think she leveled every stock accusation I had ever heard about churches and preachers in general. I loved my church and Steve Hill, and it hurt me to hear someone talk about them that way. It was especially painful because I had talked so much to my friend about God and religion and about her desire to "live right" for months before her visit to the revival. Despite all that, when it came down to making a concrete decision, her answer was, "No, I'm going to stay in sin, go to church, and still call myself a Christian."

Later on, I saw my friend and her daughter on their way out to eat at the beach. (In reality, Mom was going to drink.) Her daughter was wearing tight jeans and a halter top, looking like she was ready for action. My heart was heavy for both of them, especially for the young teenage girl who, just a few months earlier, had still possessed a precious innocence when they had both attended the Brownsville revival. That day I was heartbroken to see that the girl's innocence was gone.

Another time, I brought a friend named Mike to the revival. I knew without a doubt that he would go down to the altar and that he would never look back. I had met him just before Hurricane Opal hit Pensacola, a few months before he came to the revival. We had spent lot of time together talking about God. He had been heavily involved in drugs and the bar scene all his adult life, but during our friendship, he made it a point to stay out of that life. He was trying everything to turn his life around—from health food to self-help books. At that time, we were both trying to get over broken personal relationships, so we made a good "team." We had a lot of fun shocking everyone with our mismatched appearance—him with his long hair, and me with my general air of yuppie, mid-life crisis snobbishness.

On a Tuesday night, I told him about the revival, and he said, "Well, let's go right now." I explained that the actual revival services didn't start until Wednesday night, and that Tuesday nights were reserved for intercessory prayer meetings. Even though I explained to him that the prayer meetings were "big-time Pentecostal," Mike almost talked me into taking him with me to the prayer meeting, but he settled for waiting until the next night. He told me, "Well, if it turns out you don't go, I'll go by myself. Just tell me where it is."

I believe Steve Hill could have "served oatmeal mixed with spinach and hog jowls" that night, and it really wouldn't have mattered. Mike was ready. He was the first one to the altar, exactly as I knew he would be. When I looked down at his long, blond hair glistening in the floodlights, I also knew he had finally come home too. I went down to congratulate him and saw that his eyes were red from crying. I could tell by the look on his face that his commitment was "as tough as nails." Come hell or high water, he would never allow sin to beat him down again. From day one, Mike just kept on trucking. He witnessed to everything that breathed, was in church every minute the doors were open, and dragged his two teenage boys and anyone else he could find into church by the ears, whether they liked it or not.

Interestingly enough, the boys liked it after a while (although admitting it was another story). They couldn't help but have their spirits tenderized by such a God-filled atmosphere. I think they both went to the altar every night they were there for six months. They wouldn't fill out a decision card or anything, but they told the altar workers, "Hey, I felt like I needed to be down here. My dad keeps bringing me in here, and I keep feeling like I need to get down here." They began to call me for rides to church when their dad couldn't make it home in time to take them. Best of all, I started hearing from all the kids I knew about how much the boys had changed.

I broke into tears during almost every altar call during those first few weeks. Many times I wondered if I should be searching my own heart, but I just felt an overwhelming sorrow for friends who had come to the revival and hadn't come back. I knew the enemy of their souls had a grip on them, and I pleaded to God to touch them wherever they were and bring them home to Him. For more than a year before I came to the revival, the yuppie nightlife had sucked me in with its promises of friendship and fun. So when Steve called backsliders home during the altar calls, I knew firsthand about the deadly trap of giving up more and more holy ground until finally you're doing things you thought you would never do.

I too had allowed a web of deceit to be woven around my heart and mind, and that web was rooted in the belief that God did not have my best interests in mind. I can still remember the chilling day I stopped believing God loved me. I actually had never really grasped the concept anyway, but on that day I let the ruthless claws of self-pity, fear, and bitterness rob me of my life-source: my prayer life.

I thought, *God, if You were really there, You wouldn't have allowed me to give every minute of 13 years of my life to a lie. You wouldn't have allowed me to be deceived all along that way by man and his false doctrine. If You do exist, I can't trust You, so I had better start running away as fast as I can before You catch up with me.* I put my hands over my ears during that time of crisis, and I decided it was time that I started to take care of myself. I heaped on myself as much "feel good" religion and "get-in-touch-with-your-feelings" psychology as I could get my hands on. What a mistake that turned out to be! Now at the revival, by the mercy of God, I was hearing God's Word again and loving every minute of it.

Steve Hill sometimes classifies his messages as "honeycomb sweet"; "brussels sprouts bitter"; or "somewhere in-between." But one thing is clear: By the time the altar call is given, hearts will be either racing or resigned. Brother Hill boldly challenges church-goers to search their hearts and their lives:

"Religious person, do you wake up in the morning with Jesus on your heart? Do you think about Him all day long? Is He your very best friend? Backslider, are you doing things you thought you would never do? Is the fire gone out? Religion is hanging *around* the cross; Christianity is *getting on the cross*! Backslider, come home! You can go to hell with baptismal waters on your face or with minister's credentials on your wall. God doesn't see your church membership card—the only one He sees is blood-stained and red. One day the precious Savior will become a severe Judge! Jesus loves you and has a plan for your life!"

Each night, I watched people steadily stream from the balcony and down every aisle, and I prayed and cried with all my strength. I cried hardest for all those I knew were still wrapped up in doing things their own way instead of God's way. I knew that many of the people I had met during my days away from God wore phony glitter and partied all night on Saturday, yet they would still walk into church on Sunday morning as if everything were okay. I knew them, and I knew enough about the way they lived to understand some of their pain. I wanted so very much for them to be set free. I wanted them to see that money, popularity, and the world's myth of finding "Mr. or Mrs. Right" would never fill their emptiness. I wanted their spiritual eyes to be opened so they could see that it was all just a trick. The truth was that no matter how many people came their way or how much alcohol they drank, their pain would still be there the next day because Jesus Christ was not reigning in their lives.

I thought of all the yuppies sitting on the bleachers at my children's sports games who drove their families to church every Sunday morning. Their lives and conversations indicated they never gave God a thought—unless they thought they could get something out of it. I thought of all the forms of psychology and Eastern religion they were using to drown out the gentle voice of God. They would do anything to smooth away any hint of conviction of sin. Then I thought of all the haughty, belligerent mockers I knew. Most of them were totally different people beneath their hard bitter shells. In their honest moments, they would admit that they didn't think they were good enough to ever be touched by God.

Regardless of their walk of life, the pain they carried, or the hardness of their heart, God has used

Steve's messages and his persistent altar calls to reach the hurting and the lost. Night after night, month after month, I witnessed this evangelist's struggles to assure everyone "within the sound of his voice" that anyone without Jesus Christ as the center of his life was on his way to hell. He exempts no one when he declares each night, "If there is any doubt as to whether Jesus is first and foremost in your life, then you had better get it straight now, before it is too late!"

More than once, I've heard young people say that they were harassed so much by family or friends that they finally agreed to come to the revival. Most of them were confident that since they had been around church for so long, they could easily resist anything that was said and leave the revival unchanged. Evidently things didn't work out the way they had planned. For most of them, God either moves them to tears during praise and worship, or He breaks through their stubbornness and puts the fear of God into them during the message and altar call! In any case, I think most people end up getting a lot more than they counted on.

Many first-time visitors come to the revival to "check it out," criticize, or get someone off their back, but they ultimately end up finding life, and that more abundantly.[2] Later in the meetings, when Pastor Kilpatrick and Brother Hill begin to invite ministers and church people to come forward to receive an anointing for ministry, these same people come forward by the thousands. I noticed that more than half of the ministers, perhaps even three quarters of them, end up at the altar for repentance. Their motives for coming no longer matter as their hearts soften before God's Spirit and they begin to experience His powerful presence and anointing. As for me, my journey in God was just beginning in those early months at the revival. God assured me that He had a plan for my life and that what lay along the way would prove to be quite an adventure.

Endnotes

1. See Isaiah 55:12.
2. See John 10:10.

Chapter 5

Free Indeed

My personal path to wholeness began in earnest several weeks earlier when I went to the altar for the first time after years of pain and hardness. I had decided at the revival to "get in line behind Jesus." I knew I had to go down to the altar, but it seemed like such a long way. And I would have to go down in front of everyone no less.

Evangelist Steve Hill ministers in the revival services, which run from Wednesday night through Saturday night of each week, and Pastor Kilpatrick ministers on Sunday mornings. True to form, on Sunday mornings I always sat in the back of the Brownsville Assembly sanctuary. It may sound strange, but I felt like it was "the Brownsville people's church." In my mind, I was just a stranger at somebody else's house for breakfast. Everyone else was dressed to the hilt and talking quietly to one another before church, but I felt isolated. Although I was the one creating the "isolation," I honestly wondered if they liked new people or not, especially women with blond hair.

Delivered From Oppression

The first time I attended a Sunday morning service at Brownsville Assembly, I wore a black jumper that extended nearly to my knees. The following Sunday I decided that if I was going to do it, I might as well do it right. I decided to break from my casual yuppie tradition and wear one of my long dresses left over from days gone by. (I had donated most of my horrible, lifeless dresses and outfits to charity a few months earlier, but I had kept what few items were somewhat "stylishly conservative.") When I walked into church that morning wearing a long dress for the first time, one of Mike's teenage boys giggled and said, "You look like a schoolmarm or something, but I guess you look all right like that."

I thought to myself, *I'm different now. This is a part of me that you haven't seen before. It's a part of me I kept hidden because I was ashamed.* But some good things were there just the same, waiting to be brought out again. A healing started at that moment. I received a flicker of understanding and hope that someday I would be able to look at everything I was and had gone through—even the things I had buried and tried desperately to forget—and be in total peace.

That morning Pastor Kilpatrick stepped into that prophetic mode again, and he asked everyone who had some sort of oppression in their lives to come down to the altar area after he had preached on "The Dichotomy of a Satanic Attack." I didn't like the idea of sharing my problems with anyone on the platform, let alone in front of all those people in the pews; yet I felt I needed to be honest. I wasn't going to take any chances because I was determined to get help from God. (Little did I know that in the not-too-distant future I would be writing about much more than I could even face privately that morning.)

I waited until 50 or so people went forward (obviously believing in the "safety in numbers theory") before I apprehensively walked down the aisle. With each step, I pushed my way through great emotional waves of vulnerability and fear. I knew I had to keep on walking because I desperately wanted to be free. I was glad when two more rows of people responded to the call and came down to the front behind me. I felt more insulated and shielded with people standing in front of and behind me. I was also comforted by seeing so many others admit to having the same kind of struggles.

Pastor Kilpatrick prayed that each of us would be set free from every oppression and satanic attack that came to steal our joy and peace and hinder our personalities. He spoke words of freedom over us, and I hoped it would work. I was glad I had come forward. I figured I had a better chance of receiving help by being humble, honest, and obedient than by staying back in my seat bound by my pride and fear of the opinion of man. (In fact, I knew I had a better chance this way; I just wondered how much better those chances would be.)

After that, Lindell Cooley and the praise team began to sing, "I've Been Delivered." I didn't feel anything dramatic going on, but I got kind of a kick out of acting like I did. I jumped up and down, singing, "The hold the devil had on me, he ain't got no more." The strange thing was that the more I jumped up and down, the more I felt like I really had been delivered from oppression. Naturally, the more I felt like I had been set free, the happier I became. Finally, I was jumping up and down because I really *was* happy I'd been delivered! Everyone else was jumping around too. I even saw the lady with the Pentecostal bun waltz by. Then a lady from the praise team named Hazel kind of scooted across the front with some streamers. I quickly closed my eyes because the idea of being up front and dancing around like a mad woman suddenly became embarrassing. But a part of me wanted to continue what I was doing because I was happy and wanted to express it, so I closed my eyes. Like a little child, I figured that if I couldn't see them, then maybe they couldn't see me either.

Then the music team switched to the song that states (I don't remember the title), "We will dance on the streets that are golden, the glorious bride and the great Son of man." In my mind's eye, I could see all of us dancing on streets of gold and in a large banquet room in Heaven with Jesus. I really couldn't imagine Jesus very well, but I could almost sense His presence there. My faith was being built to an astounding level as we rehearsed the scene of the soon-coming heavenly celebration described in the Book of Revelation, the great feast called the marriage supper of the Lamb. Just as I turned my thoughts to the moment Jesus will be joined with His Bride, the Church, I opened my eyes and saw looming above me a splendid banner announcing, "The Bridegroom Cometh."

Dumbfounded, I stared at the sight of that huge, shimmering banner being carried across the front of the altar. Hundreds of people waltzed around and swayed as the song described the multitude of "every tongue and tribe and nation" that would be at this approaching heavenly celebration. I muttered aloud, "Whoa!" If I had been a hippie, I would have said, "Now, that's heavy!"

One of the scriptural references this song is based on comes from Revelation 19:

Let us be glad and rejoice, and give honor to Him: for the marriage of the Lamb is come, and His wife hath made herself ready. And to her was granted that she should be arrayed in fine linen, clean and white: for the fine linen is the righteousness of saints. And He saith unto me, Write, Blessed are they which are called unto the marriage supper of the Lamb (Revelation 19:7-9a).

In that moment, I was so thankful to be a part of the celebration. No one would ever again be able to deceive me with the shallow pleasures of tinsel town or dead religion. My sights were set on that heavenly celebration, and I was glad for the joy God would grant in between. Sunday mornings would never again be the same for me. I began to look forward to seeing what God would do next. Revival had been fun, but this was glorious. I had never experienced "glorious" before. And I was sure glad I hadn't stayed back in my seat.

Single-Focused Surrender

God dealt strongly with me about waiting for Isaac and not "settling for Ishmael" during one of Pastor Kilpatrick's piercing sermons about the dangers of not waiting on God to bring the right partner for you. When he warned us not to settle for something that was less than God's best, He seemed to be speaking directly to me. He explained that any prospective marriage partner who was not God's best and perfect will for your life would be an Ishmael. He also referred to Sister Brenda Kilpatrick's testimony of how she had been afflicted for years by attacks from a "spirit of Jezebel" that had stolen her confidence and made her afraid of what people thought. When he described that spirit of Jezebel as "a spirit of control," my eyes began to open.

The next day the Lord led me to read Proverbs 31. He spoke to my heart and said that a lot of Ishmaels would come my way but that He had someone handpicked for me. He strongly impressed upon me the idea that I was to act like I was already married, like my earthly husband was a minister who was out of town. Every single person knows that the surrender of that area of your life to God brings a lot of freedom. An incredible burden lifts once you recognize that you don't have to look for the "right" person. Christian singles are well aware of the amount of stress and distraction that can go into wondering if the "right" person is sitting on the other side of the church, and into fearing that you might miss him or her.

With that surrender, I was freed of something that may be even more important. As I thought of the ways my behavior needed to change if I were to walk in holiness, God showed me how "flirting" could be used by an oppressive Jezebel spirit to exert power and control over the attention and emotions of whomever I was flirting with! Now that was an eye-opener and an embarrassing revelation, even though the only ones in the room at the time were me and God! (That room has gotten quite a bit bigger now that it contains me, God, and everyone who reads this book.)

I must confess that I had become quite an attention seeker in my quest to fill the voids and insecurities in my life. I hated dating because it was embarrassingly artificial and stressful, but "baiting attention" had been a different story. In that moment before God, I took on the serious responsibility of not being a stumblingblock to men by being inconsiderate about how I dressed and acted.

I threw away every short dress or skirt I owned, along with everything that was too tight. I normally donate my unwanted clothes to charity organizations, but I didn't want to be responsible for someone else wearing my "Jezebel-spirit clothes." I kept my jeans but decided to wear my shirts loose without tucking them in, especially at revival. I decided not to leave any possibility that I might distract anyone from keeping his mind fixed on God. When I thought about it that way, I realized my responsibility in this area was a pretty important one.

When my male acquaintances asked me why I was always so careful not to sit by them in church services, I explained to them how God had told me to act like I was married to a minister who was out of town. That led to a long-running joke every time any of them walked up to me, "Oh, excuse me, I forgot you're an old married lady and your husband's out of town." I just smiled and answered, "Yep."

At first, it was hard to figure out how to keep my God-given, but kind of goofy, personality while I was trying to conform to this new information. I decided I would get it right after a while; but at first I thought it better to err on the side of caution, and I spent quite a bit of time by myself. The other single people I met thought I was a little stuck-up and paranoid, but I felt following God's direction needed to be my priority until I worked it all out.

The day God told me He had handpicked someone for me, I also knew I had to say good-bye to someone I had been in love with for about two years. We had dated for about a year, and our relationship had plateaued at the point at which we either had to get married or break up. He had chosen to break up, but I had chosen to "hang on." I just couldn't seem to let him go, mostly because I couldn't see how we could be so in love and it not be of God. Since neither of us dated anyone else for about a year, I and others who knew us thought it was only a matter of time before he would surrender his independence. Things became more complicated again when we went to revival together a few times. The difficult dynamics of our relationship, when put together with our life-changing commitments to the Lord, became a real distraction.

When God spoke to my heart about Ishmael through Pastor Kilpatrick's message and Proverbs 31, I finally realized I had to say good-bye. He wasn't home when I called, so I left a message on his answering machine saying that for the first time in my life, I knew that he was not the one for me. I had to sever my ties to him so God could prepare me for the one He had chosen for me and for whatever His will was for my life. I encouraged him to keep going to the revival, but I said I could not go with him or sit with him anymore.

Later that night, my girlfriend called. She said my old boyfriend had called to tell her that this time he knew his relationship with me was really over. He knew me well enough to know that if I didn't believe it was God's will for our relationship to continue (which is something we had discussed a lot even before the revival), then it was truly over. For the first time, I was not afraid of being alone. (And for the first time, I realized I really wasn't alone.)

Two days later, another friend of mine named Susan told me about a dream she had that confirmed my decision. I can't share it all, but in her dream I had invited Susan and another woman, along with a tall man dressed in a dark suit, over to a house to see a stained-glass window. She said everyone was dressed up for the occasion as I escorted them to the side of the house to see the window. Next to the window was a strong oak tree. She said I told the three people the story of how I had searched my whole life for each pane, and how now they had all been put together to form that beautiful window. A strong beam of light came through the window and caused all of the colors in the window to glow brilliantly.

In this dream, as we admired the elements of my life's work, I suddenly burst into tears in front of my guests because my love was not there to share that moment with me. Susan said she dreamed that the tall man in the dark suit put his arm around me and said, "All you have to do is walk away." In the weeks that followed, when I felt sadness or fear begin to float in my direction, I repeated the words of that dream over and over, "All you have to do is walk away." As time passed, I had to say it less and less until I finally didn't have to say it at all. I was comforted by the knowledge I had received from God through the dream that my life had not been a waste. He had brought together all the unique talents and gifts I had been given over the years so they could now shine through me and bless others.

Two months later, Susan came with me to the Brownsville revival for the first time. When Pastor John Kilpatrick walked onto the platform, she suddenly became unusually agitated and asked, "Who is that man?" She stared at him throughout the service, and it was pretty obvious she was distraught. A few days later Susan told me, "Pastor Kilpatrick was the man in the dream I told you about. He was the one who told you that all you had to do was 'walk away.' " She explained that the reason she had waited so long to tell me about it was that she didn't understand the connection. She had been really bothered in the first place just by having a dream that was so obviously symbolic for someone else. Then when she actually saw the man in her dream in person, it really threw her. I thought it was wonderful that Pastor Kilpatrick was the man in the dream. It was so like God to give my friend a dream like that since pastors are truly shepherds and protectors sent by the Lord. I was glad I had a pastor after the heart of God. In all fairness, though, visions and dreams were more out of the ordinary for Susan's personal experience than they were for mine. I found that her rather dumbfounded agitation about all this was actually sweet.

Living in Godly Humility

When I went back to church that week after receiving all the new "Jezebel/Ishmael revelations," I carefully steered clear of drawing attention to myself. I discovered that my motives were now changed. I was glorifying God instead of myself. I found myself praying for other people who were being loud and overly demonstrative—like I had been. I knew what it was like to not really be talking to the person in front of you, but rather, to everyone else within earshot. Whenever I saw this going on, I asked myself, "Was I really that oblivious?" I understood the compulsive drive for approval that can be so strong that you feel you need the approval of everyone around you. Usually it is closely linked with a strong element of rebellion that says, "You can either like my obnoxiousness, or lump it!" The mix doesn't sound like it works, but the two perfectly complement and compound one another, producing self-centeredness.

Pastor Kilpatrick continued to minister a series of messages on "The Dichotomy of a Satanic Attack" in the weeks to come, and I saw even more components of the Jezebel spirit's oppression in my life. I learned that the controlling spirit of Jezebel can come in many forms. Although I had to be careful not to control others, I also needed to get free of being her victim. For me, the former was easier than the latter. It would take some time before I finally figured out how I had become a victim of Jezebel's oppressive ways.

I immediately caught on to my tendency to want to point out everyone's faults to them. Most of the time I should have remained quiet and let God deal with my brothers and sisters, but somehow I always found it hard to "bite my tongue." Hard or easy, the Lord wanted me to let others be free, just as I had to realize my own freedom to worship and to grow in the Lord.

Soon after that, Brother Steve Hill delivered a message entitled "Counterfeit Christianity." I think I held my breath throughout the whole thing! He painted a graphic picture of the way "counterfeit Christianity" is marked by service to God in drudgery because you think you *must* serve Him to avoid being damned to hell forever. Then he explained the truth revealed in God's Word. In true Christianity, you serve God joyfully because you *want* to and because you love Him.

I had lived under the stifling bondage of counterfeit Christianity for years, and a number of individuals from my past were still trying to beat me up with it by telling me that because I had fallen away from God I did not deserve a second chance at life, or even deserve to go to

Heaven. Yes, I had "fallen away," but at long last I was living and serving God freely and happily. For the very first time, I was *living*! No one could ever again threaten my faith or my belief that I had eternal life in Christ. My joy was fully defended, and the devil and his devices had been thoroughly exposed!

That message also reassured me regarding my true motives for telling people about Jesus Christ and inviting them to church and the revival. I had a genuine desire to help free others from oppression, not some twisted desire to put them into the same Jezebel-controlled religious bondage I had once experienced. At one time, I had more faith in my personal willpower and my ability to force it on others than I had in the love and gifts of God. Then, I had wanted people to come to the Lord for my glory, not God's. I had wanted them to "stay in my church" for my glory, not due to any virtues of love or mercy.

As I noted earlier, I had been taught for many years that all ministries outside my own circle were evil and misguided. Everyone in our cultic "church" was bound safely together and rigidly manipulated in a man-controlled box. We were all bound (in the true sense of the word) to one another by the influence of a Jezebel (or controlling) spirit, by the bands of false religion, and especially by fear. I had spent 13 years of my life in a cult. When I finally discovered the true love of God and began to read anointed books outside of the carefully controlled and "approved" reading environment of the cult leaders, I (and anyone else who dared to seek to know God beyond the established legalistic structure) was repeatedly threatened, intimidated, and verbally abused. Finally, I became so confused by the harassment and conflicting messages that I became afraid. I just became quiet and gave up.

In the years before I was set free in the revival, I stopped telling anyone about God because I didn't want anyone to go through what I was experiencing. Now that I was free I could tell everyone about God with confidence and pride. (I even had a *safe place* to bring them to hear the Word of God preached in truth.)

It had been a long time since I had allowed myself to think about the things from my past. Only one year earlier, psychologists had diagnosed me with "post-traumatic stress syndrome," a stress condition similar to what POWs sometimes suffer after enduring the constant and long-term stress of enforced isolation and abuse. Just two years before, I had been on the verge of hospitalization. In my effort to hold on I pretended like the past had never happened. Now as I looked at it, I realized I could face the pain of my past with confidence. I was genuinely happy because I knew at last that I was truly free. I also knew through Christ's help I would someday forgive myself.

Chapter 6

Healing Waters

You would think that the process of forgiving myself would be a long, drawn-out one that would take years of counseling. In fact, that's what conventional wisdom says, but it didn't happen that way for me. Instead, God brought me healing through a vision.

Defeating Goliath and His Sons

During one Sunday morning service, Pastor Kilpatrick preached a message about Goliath's sons. "Many times after we conquer one spiritual 'Goliath,' or giant obstacle in our lives, we may think it is time to rest," he said. "Be on guard!" he warned. "Goliath has sons!"

I was experiencing some social pressures in the church at that time involving issues beyond my control. Just when I thought everything was finally over, rumors would seem to rise up again. All I had to keep me going was God and my children. I only wanted to live my life in peace. I cried hard throughout most of the message, but then Pastor Kilpatrick said something about rising up and taking authority over our obstacles in the name of Jesus and defeating Goliath's sons. That was when I stopped crying. It was time to face my giant and his sons; my destiny as a deliverer was waiting.

When I got home that day I declared all-out war. I rebuked every foul spirit I could think of in the name of Jesus. I marched back and forth across the floor of my house commanding satan to be bound, cast down, and cast out from every situation in my life by the blood of Jesus, and in His holy name. I backed him up against and out of every door in my house. After about a half hour of aggressive prayer and declaration according to God's Word, I fell to my knees in exhaustion and worshiped God.

This may seem strange to some, but almost immediately God gave me a "full-motion" vision. He had given me visions to guide and encourage me before, but never one that had moved like a motion picture. In this vision, I saw two people running through a forest. Somehow I knew I was the person in front. As long as I kept my eyes on the path and did not get distracted by the trees, I could keep both of us on the path. We ran faster and faster until the forest of trees began to thin out. Suddenly a tall, thin grizzly bear began to pop up and growl at us—first on one side of the path, then the other.

As I ran I kept shouting, "I rebuke you, satan, in the name of Jesus!" Each time I rebuked the bear, it dropped back down into the bushes. Then it would pop up again further down the path on the opposite side. I thought it was odd that the person behind me never helped me rebuke the bear, but I just kept running and rebuking the bear until powerful white horses came up underneath us. Suddenly we discovered our bodies were covered with the armor of medieval knights.

Without warning we came to a clearing and the other person stopped following me. Just as I was about to leave the clearing, I looked back and saw the rider start to circle around as if he or she didn't know which way to go. The rider's armor started to fall off, and when the facial shield on the helmet popped up, I realized the rider was actually a little boy.

Instantly my view shifted away from the boy and back to the armored figure of myself at the edge of the clearing. When the facial shield popped open on my figure, I immediately recognized myself as a little seven-year-old girl.

I continued to watch the confused scene in the clearing and the little innocent girl who was actually me. I began to cry and pray: "Please help her, God. Please help her find her way." I later realized that when I cried for that little girl, I was crying for myself.

My crying became an agonized heaving, moaning, and wailing—the heart language of bereavement and loss. It welled up from the deepest crevices of my soul. I wailed for all the searing pain I had suffered while trying to find my place and undergo such a radical repair of my church life. Then I moaned from deep within for all the fracturing and pain I had suffered through broken and severed personal relationships over the years. My shoulders heaved as I wept, and deep groans rose from even deeper within my being for all the crippling abuse I had endured during my 13 years of bondage in the religious cult in California. With each heave, groan, and wail, the Holy Spirit literally pulled the pain right out of my heart. Despite the pain, I kept repeating, "God, take it all! Please, take it all out of me."

Finally, I began to cry more softly, like a little girl. I was crying over all the pain I had suffered as a child. When it was all over, my body curled into a fetal position on the floor, completely enveloped in the sweet peace of God. Then I softly whispered, "Lord, I have nothing, and I am nothing." At that moment I was taken into the *shekinah* glory of God. I felt a formation of atoms floating around in His indescribable glory.

I knew that I had been taken in the spirit into the *shekinah* glory of God because a couple of days earlier a Pentecostal lady I met at church had told me, "When you are taken into the *shekinah* glory of God, nothing exists but God." It seemed odd for her to mention that because it seemed unrelated to anything else we were talking about. I had thought, *That was sure odd for her to bring that up.* I didn't have a clue of what she was talking about; I thought she was just being kind of weird. Yet as soon as I got up off the floor that night, I remembered what she had said. God had given me that information days in advance to prepare me for the vision and the experience of such a life-changing encounter with Him. He knew all along He would use it to deepen my understanding later. What had at first seemed like foolishness later became part of my own intimate experience with God. The minutes and hours I spent lost in the healing Spirit of God brought me into an intimacy with Him I could not have comprehended otherwise.

In addition to bringing me personal healing, this "moving vision" from God also contained a number of powerful teaching components. First, it told me to keep fighting no matter how many times Goliath popped up to growl at me and my family. Second, it warned me to keep my eyes on the path before me and not to get distracted by the things around me. Third, I was warned to never be dismayed or alter my course because of the confusion of others. Fourth, I learned I could only fight for others for so long. Ultimately, they will either take the responsibility of fighting the Goliaths themselves or they will get distracted from the path and be left behind. I have heeded these warnings time and time again.

Later on, I saw many believers who failed to fight their own personal Goliaths, and they missed out on their opportunities to become deliverers—at least until they came full circle and faced their giant the second time around. I could almost predict in advance that the things they were seeking and hoping for would not happen because some area of their flesh was not yet conquered. Like young David before us, every deliverer in Christ will ultimately have to fight firsthand the bears and lions who come to steal, kill, and destroy us. These enemies of our soul will test our faithfulness and willingness to sacrifice the very core of our lives for the love of God and the work of the ministry. If we succeed, God will send us to deliver others in the power of Jesus' name.

Whether we choose to fight or go with the flow and ultimately return to what is comfortable and familiar—it all hinges on obedience. Are you living a life of daily self-denial, weeding out the things that are not pleasing to God as the Spirit reveals them? When we fail, or refuse to immediately weed out something that is wrong or harmful, God will put His spotlight on it. He knows that problem will send down roots and quickly take an even stronger hold on our hearts until it begins to choke out our faith. Jesus warned His disciples, "And that which fell among thorns are they, which, when they have heard,

go forth, and are choked with cares and riches and pleasures of this life, and bring no fruit to perfection."[1]

It is the fighters who become deliverers, and it is the
deliverers who are ultimately proved faithful for greater,
more mature, and more gifted ministry work. Pastor Kilpatrick later preached a sermon that described the people
God calls to be deliverers. He explained that the obedience David exercised in stepping out in faith to slay the
bear and lion to deliver his earthly father's sheep pre-
pared him for the greater confrontation with Goliath.
That marked the beginning of his deliverance of his heavenly Father's sheep. Pastor Kilpatrick has taught many
times that before every great blessing there is a Goliath
that must be conquered first.

Personal Freedom and Obedience

I made a personal decision to never be one of those
who wandered around in the desert of doubt without ever
entering into the Promised Land. The heart of our unbelief is rooted in our fear of laying down our lives. God's
best for us awaits us in the Promised Land, not the wilderness, but *the Promised Land can only be taken in the
war of faith*. In each battle we must be obedient and yield
to His voice by laying down our lives and our ways of doing things, time and time again. We must, with the weapons of spiritual warfare, fight for all that is rightfully
ours in Christ. We must arm ourselves with the Word of
God and *use* it.

> *While it is said, Today if ye will hear His voice,
> harden not your hearts, as in the provocation. For
> some, when they had heard, did provoke: howbeit
> not all that came out of Egypt by Moses. But with
> whom was He grieved forty years? was it not with*

them that had sinned, whose carcasses fell in the wilderness? And to whom sware He that they should not enter into His rest, but to them that believed not? So we see that they could not enter in because of unbelief (Hebrews 3:15-19).

Brother Steve Hill urges us to live in obedience and courage so that when we reach Heaven we will be able to look martyrs in the face without shame because we were not cowards in the faith. These martyrs were described by John the apostle in the Book of Revelation: "And they overcame him by the blood of the Lamb, and by the word of their testimony; and they loved not their lives unto the death."[2]

That night I had my vision, I forgave myself. And I immediately noticed a change in my behavior and in my actions. I first noticed a change in how I gave my testimony. Instead of saying how horrible I had been, I talked about myself and my past in a loving way. I talked about myself and my past in a forgiving way. I talked about myself and my past in a way that spoke of God's love to me all along. I spoke of myself as though I was that little girl in the vision.

Because my view of myself was no longer one of condemnation, I also found myself loving others. When I shared the gospel with people, I saw them as children in pain and in bondage rather than as fools who needed to be won to the "right side of the tracks." After that, when I heard other Christians talk about how horrible such-and-such a group was, I would point out how the people they were talking about were people God loved but were still in darkness and needed the light of Christ in their lives. I began to share my burden to pray that satan's hold over these people would be broken so they would be set free and see clearly.

My whole perception of myself and the world was transformed. I even saw people at church differently. I no longer felt a need to change them. Accepting them became easy because I loved them much the same way I now knew God loved me. I loved them as little children. I was able to love and accept others where they were because I now loved myself.

In the months that followed, I often ran into people who had known me during the period I had been trying to serve God and the world at the same time. They usually said things like, "We were so sickening, going to church on Sunday and reading our Bibles after hanging out with such crud on Saturday night." However, instead of agreeing and condemning myself, I now said, "You know, God had His hand on us that whole time, and that was part of the process of bringing us back into His Kingdom."

One girlfriend constantly made statements like that about herself. Finally I told her, "You know, you really need to forgive yourself and see yourself through the forgiveness and love of God." When I recounted the number of times I had heard her verbally knock herself down (and me in the process), she was shocked. Then I reminded her, "...Out of the abundance of the heart the mouth speaketh" and "For as a man thinketh in his heart, so is he."[3]

I also told my friend that when she included me in those statements it made me feel like satan was reaching out and grabbing me by the throat, saying that I still had crud hanging all over me and that I was not worthy to be blessed as a child of God. We both learned from our experience, and I found I was able to be around her more often after that. Eventually we became good friends again.

Standing Ground Against Goliath

Many months later, I again encountered my "Goliath" in the area of forgiving the past and living victoriously in Christ. A certain woman overheard someone telling me how blessed she had been by a newspaper account of my testimony. When the woman heard this comment, something in her spirit rose up. She raised her finger and held it just inches from my face while saying, "Do you remember how before you came to Brownsville you didn't want anything to do with revival when I had told you about how my life had changed?" She waved her arms like she was shouting to the housetops and raved about how I had not wanted anything to do with God back then because I had wanted to do things my own way. When she put her finger in my face the third time, I said, "Please! Don't point your finger at me."

She then spun around to demonstrate how I had turned away and not wanted to hear anything about God. Once again, she put her finger in my face as if to defy my request not to point her finger at me, and she shook her head in what seemed like disgust. I quietly said, "I had a lot of pain then, and I was not yet able to face coming to God. Nevertheless, He planted His seeds along the way. We never know what a person is going through. That is why we need to be so careful about how we treat people."

I walked away feeling as if somebody had just shot me in the heart. Yes, the conversation she referred to had taken place in a parking lot one year before as she had described it. It had seemed to be a very peaceful discussion that I had actually forgotten about. I couldn't understand what her point could possibly be. I doubted that she even knew why she had acted that way.

A few minutes later as I drove home from church, I stood my ground against attacks on my mind designed to break the flow of God's joy and peace in my life. I prayed that God would give rest and forgiveness to the woman who had unknowingly hurt me so deeply. Then I began to meditate on the truths of God's Word for comfort and reassurance:

Therefore if any man be in Christ, he is a new creature: old things are passed away; behold, all things are become new (2 Corinthians 5:17).

For I will be merciful to their unrighteousness, and their sins and their iniquities will I remember no more (Hebrews 8:12).

When God set me free to view myself in the same loving way He does, He was preparing me for the future onslaught of attacks that would come from within my own mind and from other people. When our sins are washed away in the blood of Jesus Christ, God never remembers them again. I once read that God cannot and will not remember sins that are washed in the blood of the Lamb. The only ones who remember sins under the blood are ourselves, the devil, and sometimes the members of the church. In every case, it is "illegal" or useless to bring God-forgiven sins before the Judge of all men because once those sins are under the blood, it is as if they never occurred! The Spirit of God will never beat us down with the past! Any time that happens to you, you can be sure you are dealing with the hand of the devil or the fleshly nature of man. Today, I believe that any time we testify about Christ or talk about our past, we must be ever so careful to ensure we are indeed glorifying the work of Christ.

And I heard a loud voice saying in heaven, Now is come salvation, and strength, and the kingdom of our God, and the power of His Christ: for the accuser of our brethren is cast down, which accused them before our God day and night. And they overcame him by the blood of the Lamb, and by the word of their testimony; and they loved not their lives unto the death. Therefore rejoice, ye heavens, and ye that dwell in them. Woe to the inhabiters of the earth and of the sea! for the devil is come down unto you, having great wrath, because he knoweth that he hath but a short time (Revelation 12:10-12).

God's Grace Revealed

Just about the time I thought I had my past and my emotions squared away, God started to address something new that seemed a little more difficult to deal with than the last issue. My next challenge was a very hard one for me. It began with Steve Hill's message, "God Has Been Good to You." The first time he stated that in his message, I certainly did not agree with him. That evangelist had kicked over another rock, and I didn't like what I found hiding underneath it. To be honest, I immediately began thinking of all my bad experiences. I thought to myself, *Oh, yeah, that's what you think. Now don't try to trick me into thinking otherwise. God tricked me into having a horrible life even when I was doing my best to serve Him, and I am not happy with Him at all.*

Then Brother Steve started talking about how it is only God's grace that keeps our hearts beating and that it is He who keeps us spontaneously breathing, even when we're not thinking about it. Then he said that we should be thanking God that we weren't turtles trying to get across the freeway. Well, by the time Steve finished the message, I was really mad at him. I was thankful I wasn't a turtle, but that was about it.

Mad or not, that week I kept coming to the revival, and Steve Hill kept preaching the Bible. In his next few messages, Steve reminded us of even more ways that God had been good to us. I felt guilty because I couldn't make myself feel that way, no matter how much I prayed or tried to will my way into it. I knew it was just my imagination, but during these messages, I felt as if Steve was staring me down like he'd figured out I was a big old sinner with a big bad attitude who needed to get to the altar quick. Self-justification kicked in, and I figured it was useless to go to the altar since I was "already saved." When Brother Hill looked at me during the altar calls (I was still imagining that he was singling me out from the thousands in the room), I just looked blankly right back at him, trying my best not to let on to Steve that I was having a hard time.

In my heart of hearts, I knew the dross (or waste) of my heart was coming up through the preaching of the Word and the conviction of the Holy Spirit, so I prayed to God to help me get rid of my bitterness. I confessed that it was something I could not do by myself.[4]

Finally, Steve Hill went all out and preached the message, "God Will Cut You Down." He took this message from the Lord's parable about the fig tree in the Gospel of Luke:

He spake also this parable; A certain man had a fig tree planted in his vineyard; and he came and sought fruit thereon, and found none. Then said he unto the dresser of his vineyard, Behold, these three *years I come seeking fruit on this fig tree, and find none: cut it down; why cumbereth it the ground? And he answering said unto him, Lord, let it alone this year also, till I shall dig about it, and dung it: and **if it bear fruit, well**: and **if not**, then after that **thou shalt cut it down*** (Luke 13:6-9).

Then he told the story of the fig tree that was given one more year to bear fruit before it would be cut down. Steve Hill walked around the sanctuary and even up into the balcony with a big double-headed ax in his hands. He warned the shocked people: "God will cut you down. If you're not bearing fruit, He will cut you down. This may be the end of your last year." Of course he made it clear that people who were washed in the blood and obeying God's commands had nothing to fear, but he purposely let everyone else who wasn't in that category stew in their predicament. What could I say? It was right there in God's Word.

The altars filled up quickly that night! As Steve walked up the right side of the balcony, people flushed down the stairs to the left before he even got to them. When that ax went by I looked right at it, fully confident that I was bearing spiritual fruit despite my troubled heart. At the end of the service, however, I felt like Steve hated me. I felt lonely and afraid, and I suddenly recognized it as the spirit of the condemnation of man that I had felt for so many years. I thought I had been set free from it in the last couple of weeks, but I sensed that God was allowing it to manifest so He could get rid of the root once and for all.

While altar workers were counseling people, I saw a friend of mine standing in the pews on the other side of the sanctuary. When an altar worker reached her she was "shaking." This physical manifestation was something I had tried to ignore. I'd seen people's hands, or heads, or whole bodies shaking—anywhere from a bit to pretty radically—during the services and during prayer time. One friend I brought to the revival said, "I have never seen so many people in the same room with the *same disorder* in my life." I busted out laughing, and I told her that it was a manifestation of the power of God touching them and that His power is so strong that human bodies can't take it and they often end up shaking. (If mountains and temples shake under the power of God, then it would certainly be true of little people.) My friend wasn't sure how to respond to that. She looked at me like we'd better drop the subject real quick.

Supernaturally Set Free

Personally, I had thought it best to ignore shaking and some of the other manifestations. I didn't understand it and figured people with major problems probably shook. I had also heard about the Alison Ward video in which she warned about the judgment of God and shook during the whole thing. When people all around the country and in different parts of the world would watch that video, they would feel the power of God. Many times they would start shaking and revival would then break out in their lives and in their churches. Months later, Alison explained to me that some shaking is a form of intercession, and some shaking is God touching people personally or setting them spiritually free of something. Alison further explained to me that her sister Elizabeth didn't shake much after a few months, for God had initially used shaking to show her that He was real and all-powerful.

Alison, on the other hand, continued to shake as a form of intercession, and God had used it to show other people His power.

Steve often makes reference to "manifestations" at the beginning of services, saying something like, "Hey, don't major on the minor stuff. If someone is shaking or moving their arm around funny, why don't you move a little closer to them. It may just rub off on you." I would laugh, but I would also move a little further away. That too was about to change.

I was feeling so bad after the ax message that night that I decided to take drastic measures to get rid of my bad feelings. I walked up to that friend of mine with the "radical shake" and gave her a hug. I said, "I'm having a real bad day. Give me some of that shaking stuff." She said, "Okay." She confidently grabbed my hands into hers and immediately we both began to laugh uncontrollably. I started shaking and had such holy laughter that women started coming up and grabbing our hands saying, "Give me some of that." Within a few minutes, there were about six of us women shaking and laughing.

While the six of us were laughing and standing in a circle with our hands on top of each other's like we were on a football team ready to go out and play the game, Steve walked toward us with a big smile on his face. He waved his hand at us and said something like, "More, Lord." The power of God hit us so hard that we were literally knocked in six different directions. It was like Steve had thrown a hand grenade containing the power of God.

I was thrown backward to the floor, and I ended up lying under a pew, laughing my head off. I could hear my friend's laughter echoing from somewhere under the same pew. I heard Steve chuckling as he walked by us. My fear of him was healed in that moment because I knew he had my good in mind and was sharing in and contributing to my joy. Somehow, I felt Steve and I were now on the same side and the same team. I guess God was healing my fear of men in spiritual authority. I had been confusing the devilish condemnation tactics used by leaders in the cult with the uplifting conviction of the Holy Ghost that followed Steve Hill's blunt delivery of a message direct from God's Word.

When I got up from the floor I continued to laugh for a little while. After a few minutes, I decided to find someone to pray for me. When I began to walk I started to spontaneously bow at the waist. I was still experiencing some holy laughter, so I thought it was kind of funny. When people who knew I didn't normally do that sort of thing would look at me and grin, I'd smile back at them with the expression, "Hey, don't ask me." Or I'd laugh and say, "I can't stop this."

I saw Pastor Kilpatrick at the altar praying for people so I started to follow him around, bowing and all. He never did pray for me. I think maybe he or God figured it was my bowing time. I eventually learned that bowing is a sign that someone is called to be an intercessor.

Later, I laughed and nodded my head in agreement whenever Pastor Kilpatrick said, "The surest way to stop judging manifestations is for it to happen to you." I thought, *You can say that again.* I also experienced "falling out," or "being slain in the Spirit" when people put their hands on my forehead and prayed for me. Peace swept over me, and it became hard to stand up. I fell backward and lay on the floor for a while. Sometimes during this time I would feel more pain being pulled out of my heart. I'd feel like spiritual oil was being poured over my brain, or God would show me a vision.

For a month or so after my holy laughter/bowing experience, I sometimes shook a bit when I was lying on the floor. At first, I was a little embarrassed, but I learned to trust God. I always felt a little freer and a little more confident afterward. Now when I see people shaking, I'm glad that God is touching their lives.

The next morning when the congregation prayed for the sick I again started to bow spontaneously. I didn't know why, but it seemed like it was somehow related to praying for these people because I would bow each time a name was mentioned as being in need of prayer

Pastor Kilpatrick preached that morning on "Healing of the Memories." As he made statements like, "Not all of your memories have been bad ones," I felt the oil of healing begin to flow over my heart. I began to remember the happy times of my childhood, and I dug deep to find happy memories from my adult life. When he asked everyone to come forward who needed their memories to be healed, I stepped out without hesitation. I didn't look behind me, but it seemed to me like the whole church flooded to the altar that morning. He prayed for us to be able to look back on our memories and remember happy times. He also prayed that when we would remember the hard times that we would no longer feel the pain, that instead it would be healed. I pressed in to receive all there was to receive from God from that prayer.

When I walked back to my pew, I was no longer afraid. Later that night when I drove home and walked back into my house, I realized I still wasn't afraid. I was ready to begin a life without fear and without shame.

Endnotes

1. See Luke 8:14.
2. See Revelation 12:11.
3. See Matthew 12:34 and Proverbs 23:7.
4. "Take away the dross from the silver, and there shall come forth a vessel for the refiner" (Prov. 25:4).

Chapter 7

Time for War

As I stepped into the baptismal pool perched high above the platform and the thousands of people attending the Brownsville revival that Friday night, I was glad for the smiling faces looking up at me from the choir. Their faces were beaming, and to me they looked like little angels. I was also glad to know that Pastor John Kilpatrick and Steve Hill were sitting in their chairs on the left of the platform—I figured I could look to them for moral support if I found myself in a nervous crunch.

Looking out over the auditorium, I felt like I was about to address some immense stadium crowded with people. My thoughts rushed back to the previous Sunday morning service when Pastor Kilpatrick had prayed over everyone in the building, asking God to heal our memories. In that moment, I knew I was ready to publicly bury my old life of pain in the baptismal waters and come up into newness of life. Nobody else knew why it had taken me so long to get baptized, but God and I knew.

Childhood Experiences

I had been baptized once before, when I was nine years old. The baptismal class instructor had said we didn't have to say anything, but I decided to say what was in my heart even though I knew I would stutter the whole way through. I thought God would like that. I also thought that maybe others would see how happy you can be with Jesus as your Savior. My parents and my best girlfriend, who was Catholic, sat smiling on the front row. I'm not sure anyone understood what I said because I did stutter over every word, just like I thought I would. Yet somehow I managed to laboriously get a couple of sentences out.

Hoping my girlfriend didn't think I looked too stupid, I told those big adult bodies in all those big pews that I had gone to church summer camp for a week and now that I felt closer to God than ever before, I wanted to get baptized. I could tell by everyone's smiling faces that they loved me even though I was a stutterer. As a nine-year-old girl in the baptismal pool, I pictured myself living the rest of my life with Jesus. That was to be cut short, however.

A few weeks later, my little girlfriends who rode the church bus with me to Sunday school were sexually fondled by the church bus driver. I was too frightened to get back on the bus, and I was too confused to even go back to church—even when my mom offered to take me. Although I stopped going to that church, for weeks I waited and hoped that my Sunday school teacher or the pastor would call me because I felt I could trust them. I kept asking my mom if they had called yet, and I even imagined them coming over to my house to help me. But they never came. Eventually, I realized they never would.

By the time I was ten years old, I wouldn't even attend the *Awana* Bible club that had been started at the elementary school across the street from my house in the suburbs of Chicago. With my mouth I said, "Oh, that's just stupid," but the pain in my heart kept repeating again and again, "They never came. They never cared enough about me to even call."

For years, I longed to feel the way I had as a joyful little girl talking about Jesus in that baptismal pool. Unfortunately, the walls I put up got thicker with each passing year. In the years that followed, I would sporadically hear the voice of God in answer to my prayers, even after I moved to California with my father. But I was a senior in college before I ever again heard and received the life-changing message of salvation in Jesus Christ.

Restoration of Joy

On that wonderful Friday evening at Brownsville Assembly of God in Florida, God restored my childlike heart, and once again He allowed me to rejoice with "joy unspeakable and full of glory."[1] As I looked out into the huge crowd at Brownsville, I knew my own nine-year-old daughter, who was the same age I was when I was first baptized all those years ago, was watching me closely. I knew she was proud to see her mama get baptized. I also knew my 13-year-old daughter, Rachel, was out there holding her breath for me. I wasn't too worried about stuttering in front of everyone this time. I had asked God to help me not to stutter so that I could say what He wanted me to say.

I knew better than to plan what I was going to say in advance. I've learned that He usually doesn't give you His perfect answer until the last minute. In Corrie ten Boom's book, *The Hiding Place*, she shares her father's explanation that God waits to give us what we need until the last minute before we need it, just as he, her earthly father, waited to give Corrie her train ticket until right before she was to board the train.[2] God gave me the framework and some of the words to say only moments before I stepped into the baptismal water. I never doubted that He would do otherwise.

As I stood in waist-deep water, I publicly thanked God for the privilege of being baptized at the revival at Brownsville Assembly of God. (I was really giving thanks for a dual baptism—I had been immersed in His mighty river of revival, and now I was being dunked in the waters of baptism!) Then I told the crowd how God had spoken to me in an almost audible voice in an airport in Wichita, Kansas, seven years earlier: "God had told me there would be a worldwide revival in Pensacola, Florida, and then He 'slew me in the Spirit' right there in the airport and said the words, 'Azusa Street: Pensacola, Florida; Azusa Street: Pensacola, Florida.'"

Then I explained how I couldn't find the revival anywhere after I moved to Pensacola. I told them that things became really, really hard. I confessed, "I came under a stronghold that just mixed me up so much that I began to think that the wounds of man were the wounds of God." My voice trailed off like I was trying to figure it out. Then I heard myself say, "It was just a stronghold but God set me free." I looked down toward the left of the stage, and I saw Brother Steve Hill vigorously shaking his head "yes," so I repeated the words with more confidence, "It was just a stronghold, but *God has set me free!*"

With that said, I promptly turned around the wrong way and I guess everyone clapped. I finally managed to get turned around the right way, and the last thing I remember is plugging my nose for the "dunk." Somehow I ended up standing at the top of the steps on the other side of the baptismal pool! I looked down at the people who were now in the pool and wondered, *Now how did I get up those stairs?* I felt like I had flown up there. I didn't remember climbing those steps myself. I must have been totally overcome by the glory of God, and I was without any recollection of those few moments. A few days later someone finally told me that the men who baptized me had carried me up the steps.

Once I got into dry clothes and made my way back to my seat, I noticed that the power of God had fallen on my nine-year-old, Aimee. I was alarmed by the strength of her physical manifestation. She had never done anything like this before. In fact, Aimee didn't even like for people to pray for her. That night she had her arms raised above her head, and she was bending deep at the knees and kind of running in place all at the same time! Her face was flushed and she was out of breath.

My friends who were watching her during the baptismal service seemed to think it was the sweetest thing they'd ever seen, but my motherly instinct kicked into overdrive. (I'm sharing this to let you know that I'm just as human as you are. I still wasn't totally sold on physical manifestations, even then, and I really didn't understand them.) I was concerned that Aimee would become overheated. I had no sooner dealt with that thought than another one flew in to take its place: *Aimee must be doing it to get attention.* Then I began to feel embarrassed by the next thought that came unbidden to my mind, *Everybody will think I'm not a good mom if I let her hurt herself.* Finally I sat her on my lap to make sure she was okay. I wouldn't let her stand up and even made her sit down on the pew after I stood up to sing. She seemed to calm down and just did a little bowing while seated in the pew. I figured everyone near us thought I had hindered the Spirit (frankly, now I doubt if they had even noticed), but I told myself, *I am just not ready for this and have to go with what I think best as a parent right now.*

Later on my friend told me that she had asked Aimee if she was all right earlier in the service. Aimee had told her at that time, "An angel is holding my hands and shaking all of the sin out of me."

During the praise and worship time, I tried to keep my mind on the songs, but the enemy kept battering me with fearful thoughts about what I had said in the baptismal pool, thoughts like: *You probably sounded totally stupid.* Finally, I asked a couple of people if I had sounded stupid and they told me not to be silly. "You were a real blessing!" they assured me. But I didn't believe them.

When the worship team suddenly began to sing, "I've Been Delivered," I said to myself, "I've had enough of the devil beating me up with worry. I don't care about what other people think about what I said. I've been delivered."

By the time the third line of the song rolled around, I bolted down to the altar, wet hair and all, and I started jumping up. I was singing, "The hold the devil had on me, he ain't got no more!" I don't think anybody else was down there but me, but I didn't care because "I'd been delivered."

Within a few moments, Steve grabbed the microphone and said, "I want anyone who has been delivered of something during this revival to come down here right now and sing this song!" Immediately, it looked like a big floodgate busted open and people poured down to the front from every direction—and most of them were running! I thought, *Boy, I didn't have to stay down here by myself very long.*

People were jammed shoulder to shoulder as far as I could see, stretching all the way across the altar areas and up all the aisles. We all smiled at each other until our faces ached, and we bounced up and down as we sang and rejoiced in the Lord together with unhindered joy. When the music team began to sing "Look What the Lord Has Done" the jubilation surged to such an incredible expression of victory that I felt like we were literally stomping on satan's head.

For the next few weeks, every time I heard Pastor Kilpatrick mention the word *Brownsville*, I burst into tears. It was the only way I could express my thankfulness to God for bringing me to Brownsville, and to the obedient ministry of Pastor John Kilpatrick, Steve Hill, and all the other wonderful people who had been so faithful to the call of God.

Exercising Authority

The day after my baptism, I went through my house and swept it clean of every trace of demonic oppression and worldly influence. I had learned at the Tuesday prayer meetings about the power and authority we have through the blood of Jesus Christ and in His name. I was determined to command the powers of darkness to leave every nook and cranny of my life and home.

I went through every room in my house, and then I walked around the yard, saying: "I rebuke you, satan, in the name of Jesus. By the blood of Jesus Christ you have no authority here. So every foul spirit, I command you to go into the dry places of the earth, never to return! Now go!" Then I put dabs of oil above every door and window of my house and said, "I anoint and dedicate this house and family to God Almighty in the name of the Father, the Son, and the Holy Ghost." I also asked God to send His glory and to post angels of protection around and about the house. I did the same with my car. For a long time, I did this almost daily.

I had already gotten rid of a lot of pictures and things that reminded me of sins of the past, but I was surprised at how much more I found I needed to get rid of. I found and threw out everything, from T-shirts that took me down memory lane to jewelry that might be associated with witchcraft to New Age/psychology books. I also went through my daughter Aimee's toys and books and got rid of anything associated with witchcraft. Now that was a bagful!

I also made the commitment to actually act out putting on the whole armor of God every morning,[3] just as Sister Kilpatrick had suggested. I also committed to pray each day for the Lord to bathe me and my children with the protection of His blood—from the tops of our heads to the soles of our feet like I had heard different people at church do. I figured that if were going to "plead the blood" all over the church on Tuesday nights, I sure ought to be pleading it all over myself and my children.

In Love With Jesus

March proved to be a hard month for me. A number of circumstances arose that made me feel very much alone.

I felt totally separated from the few people whom I relied on for fellowship. One night I felt so alone that I called up a friend who was no longer going to the revival, but somehow I knew the door was shut. There was no common ground left, and I had to go it alone.

I cried that night for a couple of hours, and in the midst of my loneliness I fell in love with Jesus. As I came to the end of my weeping, I knew in my heart of hearts that if the only person left on the earth was me, and if all I had was my relationship with Jesus, that I would be completely fulfilled and satisfied. Jesus was the only person I could rely on, and He was all I needed to be complete. I had often wondered what people meant when they said they had "fallen in love with Jesus." I always used to wish it could happen to me, and now it had. I had finally fallen in love with Jesus.

The next day I looked at the bottle of Prozac, the drug the psychiatrists and psychologists wanted me to use to hold my world together. Then I threw it in the trash. I knew it would be a little tough, but I also knew that with Jesus all things were possible.

That first night I went back to the revival, I had been off of Prozac for almost two days. I cried from the minute I walked in the door. I couldn't stop thinking of all my friends who had left the revival. Yet I didn't know if I was crying about them, or just crying because of a chemical imbalance due to medication withdrawal. I just cried and cried, even when the service started. I was only a few rows from the platform, but I had to sit down abruptly right in front of everyone for the first few songs. By the fourth song or so, I forced myself to stand up again and smile. Eventually I broke free in praise a little bit. On Thursday night I cried a little less, and on Friday, I cried a little less than that. By Saturday afternoon, I knew I was totally free of my Prozac dependency.

That night I jumped up and down and rejoiced because I knew nothing and no one would ever push me down again. Although I might find myself sitting on my backside with the wind knocked out of me after suffering the many disappointments due to man's failures, God has never once failed to pick me up again and defend me in greater ways than I could ever imagine. People and situations would appear like they were about to knock me off the path, but God always came down in power. And every time He has brought me back twice as strong.

Dying Daily

God has often brought to my memory the moving vision I shared in Chapter 6. One of the components He repeatedly reminded me about was that of the little "boy-knight" who followed me in the vision but never rebuked the bear that popped up on the side of the path. I saw many people around me who, for various reasons, would not fight their personal Goliaths. I knew these people were missing their destinies as deliverers. Each was a warning to me.

I could almost predict in advance what was about to happen to those who only "rode the coattails" of revival and the prayers of others. They tended to avoid facing the challenge to conquer the things defeating their lives. It seemed to me that the greatest challenge that nearly everyone faced was the call to genuine humility. Some of these people would fall back into the sins of the flesh; others returned to the wreckage of dead religion; and some simply refused to confront their fears and sins. They just kept spinning in circles because they chose to do things their own way.

Jesus said, "And they [the seeds] which fell among thorns are they, which, when they have heard, go forth, and are choked with cares and riches and pleasures of this life, and bring no fruit to perfection."[4] God calls us to live lives of self-denial on a daily basis as we weed out those things the Spirit reveals to us that are not pleasing to God. The Lord longs to see us all bear a "bumper crop" of good fruit in our lives. I was learning that good fruit came from believing the Word of God and acting on it.

For me, my children, and my fellow laborers, the biblical process of "dying daily" to self so that we might live and rejoice in Jesus Christ came to be what revival and life was all about. We were determined to enter into God's rest in every area of life.

Endnotes

1. See First Peter 1:8.
2. Corrie ten Boom, *The Hiding Place* (Fleming H. Revell, Co., 1971).
3. See Ephesians 6:11-17.
4. See Luke 8:14.

Chapter 8

Winter Ends

I came back to my seat and found my 13-year-old daughter Rachel kneeling between the pews with her face pressed against the floor! I really couldn't believe my eyes. The service that Sunday morning marked the nine-month anniversary of the start of the Brownsville Revival, and such an awesome presence of holiness had come into the sanctuary that a lot of people had actually taken their shoes off. We felt as if we were standing on holy ground. Pastor Kilpatrick never had an opportunity to preach that morning because it was clear that God was directing us to worship and adore Him.

Earlier in the service, I had felt led of the Spirit to go down to the altar to worship the Lord, and as I stood there I felt something pushing my head down farther and farther until I found myself on my knees with my face to the floor. It was as if a big hand was holding my head to the ground. I felt a little odd since this was happening at the altar right in front of people. After a few minutes, I looked a little to my right and left, and though my head was still pressed to the ground, I could see that some people at the altar were actually lying all the way down on the floor worshiping God. Obviously, something very unusual was taking place in that service.

After about 20 minutes, the force that was gently pressing us to the floor suddenly lifted and I stood up. In fact, it seemed like everybody stood up at about the same time. I stayed at the altar and worshiped the Lord during two more worship songs. Then I went back to my seat to be with my children. That is when I found Rachel kneeling between the pews.

I thought, *Whoa, God truly must be doing something amazing in this place!* (You know as well as I do that teenagers normally don't kneel in a church unless they are told to.) My 14-year-old son, Aaron, was looking a little stunned himself when he said, "Mom, something kept kicking my legs out from under me. It almost made me fall down. I thought it was the weirdest thing, and I had to hold onto the pew just to stand up. Then all of a sudden Rachel ended up on the floor."

Rachel stayed pressed to the floor for about two more songs. When she got up she seemed to be pondering what had happened to her and said, "Something kept pushing my head down further and further, and it made me kneel and put my face on the ground." I smiled and told her, "The same thing happened to me. It's so odd that the same thing happened to both of us."

Teenage Revival

I figured that if the power of God could put Rachel on her face after what she and I had been through on the way to church, then the presence of God in that place was even stronger than I had realized. Getting Rachel to church that morning had been like going through a parental torture chamber. The girl wanted to go anywhere but to Brownsville. She grunted and groaned and slipped into her teenage, slow-motion gear as she got ready. She whined and shuffled her feet as she protested, "We won't get out of there for four or five hours, and we'll have to stand and clap our hands until our arms and legs are ready to fall off. It's horrible there!"

When I wouldn't let the kids listen to rock music on the way to church, Rachel had mocked me, saying, "And now I guess all music except 'la, la, la, opera Christian stuff' is of the devil. Now Mom, if you start wearing culottes, like they do at Pensacola Christian Academy, I'm going to have a heart attack." I sensed panic in her voice. She had already come home from school to find that MTV had disappeared from the cable television selections. She was obviously becoming nervous.

The next Thursday night I asked Rachel if she wanted to go to the Brownsville youth group meeting, and she surprised me by saying, "Yes." Afterward, I asked her what she thought of it. She said, "It was pretty cool. I think I want to start going regularly." I was really relieved because I thought maybe the youth group would help me with her. She had always been a good kid, but in the last year she had been getting more and more sucked into "boy craziness," pop rock, wanting to go to dances, and non-stop gossiping. I felt like she was slipping away right before my eyes. Now, I felt like hope may be on the horizon. Maybe I wouldn't lose my daughter (to who knows what) after all. Little did I know that God was about to turn her into an on-fire teenage evangelist within just a few short weeks.

Two weeks later, Rachel found me in the sanctuary after her youth service was over. It was held in another building on the Brownsville campus. She was shaking like she had just gotten out of a cold swimming pool on a chilly day. I just couldn't believe it. The "mother" in me didn't like it much, but I didn't say anything. However, I was glad when I saw her dash off happily with her friends to get prayed for by Steve Hill who was still praying for people after the main service had concluded. Nevertheless, I still have to confess that I was a little worried about her because she was still shaking.

Rachel really surprised me when she came up to me afterward and said she wanted to go with me to revival the next night! She even invited a bunch of her friends, her brother Aaron, and her stepbrother from her father's second marriage to go along with us. That Friday night I drove a packed carload of happy campers over to the revival, and they were all excited about checking out "this thing" Rachel had told them about. After the service, Rachel told me that she had shaken like crazy through the whole service while she sat up in the balcony with her friends. Once again, I didn't like that idea at all. I half-wondered if she was doing it on purpose. I tried not to worry too much about her shaking as she and her friends giddily went off, but I didn't know what to make of it: All of them, including Aaron, seemed to think the revival was "extremely cool."

A few days later I walked by Rachel's room and overheard her talking on the phone. It was probably the first time I had ever eavesdropped, but I couldn't help myself. She was bubbly and excited as she told the person on the other end about the revival. Even more than the excitement, I sensed a genuine sense of urgency in her voice.

She was clearly trying to relay how important it was for her friend to go to the meetings. It was a mother's dream come true.

My dream continued into the week when Rachel threw out the few soft rock CDs she owned and began to ask me if I thought her dresses were too short or too revealing! My house soon became a witnessing station, and my car became a teenage transportation vehicle to the revival.

Increasing Fruit in the Children

Rachel actively participated in youth groups at two other churches as well as at Brownsville Assembly. Invariably when I would go to pick her up, she would be witnessing to someone about the need for Jesus Christ to be the Lord of every part of their lives. Of course, she'd be telling them in standard teenage lingo. She often begged me to let her stay up for just another 15 minutes so she could check on her new converts. She asked my advice regarding things like which parts of the Bible she should tell these young converts to read first and how she should handle their more difficult questions. Whenever adults asked Rachel about the change in her life, she would tell them that it really began when the power of God came on her so strongly at the revival that she began to shake. She always says that without question.

One of the sweetest things I noticed was how often Rachel would repeat things said by Brother Richard Crisco (the youth pastor at Brownsville Assembly), or how she would mention how nice he was to her and all the other kids. Several months later I went into a youth service myself. Brother Richard actually preached in his stocking feet! He had such profound honesty, humility, and love for the kids that I knew why God was moving so mightily among the teenagers. God had given them a shepherd who truly loved and cared for his young sheep. Brother Richard talked straight with the kids. He knew what they were up against and was determined to equip them with the truth and with the weapons they would need. He developed a powerful and fast-moving discipleship program that really seemed to work for the kids, and I was overjoyed to see Rachel dive into the program headfirst.

I heard that Brother Richard frequently told the teens: "I am not impressed with people who shake, or fall, or speak in tongues. I want to see a change in your lives." I saw that kind of change take place in the lives of my own teens, and I also saw it in the lives of the kids Rachel dragged to the revival. She either pestered them into giving in and going, or she would warn them about hell until they finally went enough times to grab hold of the gospel for themselves. At that point, they would begin to either call us for a ride or start getting there on their own.

Daily new stories circulated about kids I personally knew who became convicted and changed by the Spirit of God. Malicious gossips with years of experience became convicted for their sin and committed themselves to change. I constantly heard about kids who smashed ungodly CDs in their backyards and broke off their sexually active relationships. I listened to Rachel call up the biggest druggies in town—even boys who only knew her because they had played in sports with her brother—just to bug them to go to the revival. With the follow-up help from her brother and other friends in the youth group, some of these young people actually went to the revival and had their lives completely transformed.

At first, Aaron thought Rachel's zeal was just too intense for his taste. He complained to me about her witnessing too hard to everybody and always riding his case. He had always been a quiet type who didn't like to make waves, but after a while he became a support and pillar for his "ditsy for the Lord" sisters and mom.

It was always exciting to hear all the strategies the kids came up with for "twisting their friends' arms" to get them to the revival. Sometimes they even double-teamed the teens they all knew. Eventually they had four to six new kids going with them each night!

One night I heard that some teens who were notoriously steeped in drugs, alcohol, promiscuity, and rebellion had been persuaded by Rachel and Aaron's older friends to come to the revival. They came in mocking it and saying they were just there to check it out. Rachel and others who sat with them that night said every one of the boys were crying within the first half hour of the praise and worship portion that Friday night revival service. They all accepted Jesus Christ as their personal Savior at the altar, and their lives were notably changed. In later months, however, these boys wavered in the face of persecution and fell back into their old ways. We continue to pray for them. I too fell away as a child, but by His grace God brought me back home.

One of the tenderest moments I experienced occurred the night I found my little nine-year-old Aimee curled up in bed with her Bible. I thought she was in another room watching television. After that night, she often told me about how she got her little friends to pray the sinner's prayer with her. One time she said she started telling a little friend about how she needed to ask Jesus into her heart. She said the girl immediately defended herself and boldly said she was a Christian. Then Aimee told me, "But when I started telling her about how horrible hell is, she said she wasn't a Christian real fast. But she also told me she wanted to be one, so I showed her how to ask Jesus into her heart."

During the months of March and early April, Rachel was still chasing after as many people as she could find to pray for her after revival services because she had never been "slain in the Spirit." She was obviously concerned about this. One night she came up to me and said she had asked Brother Richard why she never "went out" like some of the other kids. She proudly told me that he had said, "I know a lot of kids who are slain in the Spirit, but I don't see in their lives what I see in yours." That statement touched her in a very deep way. I could tell that it both encouraged and motivated her.

From that day on, it seemed that Brother Richard became a real friend to her. Oftentimes we would be on our way to the car when she would stop in her tracks and announce something like, "Oh, I forgot to say 'hi' to Brother Richard," or "Brother Richard looked so tired tonight that I think I need to see if he's okay. Can I go say 'hi' real quick?" Although this was a bit of an inconvenience and it was usually pretty late, I would wait for her because I knew how important his support had become to her.

A Celebration of Life

For all of us, Easter weekend of 1996 was like no other we'd known. The closer we came to Good Friday, the day set aside to recognize the crucifixion of Jesus Christ, the more I would find myself sobbing. Brother Dick Reuben, a Messianic Jewish evangelist who regularly ministered at the revival, described the suffering of Jesus Christ with such detail that I could picture my Savior's agony in my mind. The Sunday before Good Friday, Brother Reuben described the crucifixion during a moving communion service, and it nearly broke my heart. Over the next few days Pastor John Kilpatrick also brought me to tears when he painted incredible word pictures of Jesus' sufferings. By the time Good Friday came, I was ready to burst into tears at the mere mention of Jesus' name. I was heartbroken over what He suffered for us, and more personally, what He'd suffered for me. All I could do was thank Him.

The Saturday night before Easter, I no longer cried when the death of Jesus was described. Instead I began rejoicing that He had conquered death and hell when He rose from the dead.

Easter morning was a spectacular day of celebration at Brownsville. The sanctuary was packed (as it always is nowadays), and everyone was dressed beautifully. Many of us were jumping up and down in front of our pews from the very first chord of the very first song!

Everyone chuckled when Pastor came out on the platform wearing a suit jacket so brilliant that he looked like an Easter egg. At one point, Brother Richard Crisco put on a pair of sunglasses to poke fun at him, but Pastor Kilpatrick had the last laugh. As he looked over at all the ministers on the platform, he said, "I came to church brightly dressed this Easter morning because I am here to celebrate. I wasn't about to wear that old black stuff— like some folks I know!" Of course, Steve Hill, Richard Crisco, and the other ministers were all wearing black suits, so it was quite hilarious. (Many people have the wrong idea that revival is always serious and somber, but true revival is truly *fun*! The presence of God brings unspeakable joy and gladness to everyone it touches.)

Pastor Kilpatrick powerfully illustrated his message when he boldly undraped three six-foot banners, one at a time, at just the right moment. Each banner that was unveiled bolstered my faith as a determined warrior for Christ, as did the Scriptures that had inspired them. The first banner symbolized "Jesus Christ, the Lion of the Tribe of Judah," and it was inspired by the passage in Revelation 5:1-5. The second banner symbolized "Jesus Christ, the Lamb of God" as described in Revelation 5:6-14. The third banner pictured Jesus riding on a white horse in His authority and power as "King of kings, and Lord of lords" as revealed in Revelation 19:11-16.

I knew in the depths of my being that I was called to be a conqueror and that all things were truly possible through Him.[1] As never before, I cleaved and bonded in faith to Jesus Christ, my victorious King. In that moment, I knew that at long last the winter of my life was over.

Endnote

1. See Mark 10:27 and Romans 8:37.

Chapter 9

Encounters With Power and Divine Appointments

I wasn't doing anything that I didn't usually do. I was worshiping the Lord like everyone else and suddenly a bolt of the power of God hit me from nowhere and threw me back into my pew. I sat there under the heaviness of the glory of God's presence for a few minutes. I was unable to open my eyes and felt a kind of peace floating from my shoulders up. It was like I was halfway slain in the Spirit.

After two or three minutes, I figured I was probably ready to stand and make an effort to participate in the songs with everyone else. I grabbed onto the pew and pulled myself to my feet. I had to brace myself by continuing to hold onto the pew in front of me in order to stand up under the heaviness of the Spirit as I sang along with my eyes closed. Within a few minutes, the bolt hit me again and threw me back down into my pew.

I was happy when Pastor Kilpatrick briefly interrupted the worship service to say something and I had an opportunity to sit down. I don't remember the context of his statement, but when he mentioned the number of souls that had been saved in the revival up to that point, I started to cry spontaneously. Then when he began a short exhortation on the need for lost souls to hear the gospel, I wept for lost souls in Pensacola and elsewhere. This continued until the Pastor changed to a different subject.

During Steve Hill's message that night, I got "bolted" by God's glory a couple of more times. My head was thrown back and I was knocked a little further into my seat. It was like God was saying "Amen" to specific points of Steve's message by hitting me with a bolt each time! I could barely focus my eyes on Steve while he preached, although I could hear everything he was saying.

Steve asked everyone in the sanctuary to stand as he encouraged people to come to the front for salvation. I obediently rose to my feet, yet the moment I stood up I was promptly knocked into the pew again. When I dragged myself back onto my feet, Steve was still calling people to come to the front for salvation. When he asked everyone to look at him, I forced my eyes open, but I could barely see him. (This was definitely not part of my agenda for that night.)

At some point in the service, I began to involuntarily bow with such quick and shallow movements that it could have been called shaking. I didn't have time to think about what anyone else thought because I was too busy trying to deal with all the physical stuff I was experiencing. To top everything off, the heaviness of the presence of God was so strong that it made me feel like I was in a bubble. Somehow throughout this process I knew I was interceding for souls to come to the altar. Each Sunday for the past month since the nine-month anniversary service, I felt that same hand pushing my head down until I bowed at the waist during the worship service and the altar call. This new manifestation of rapid, involuntary bowing seemed to come out of nowhere, just like the bolt of power that had kept hitting me.

Suddenly, I felt cramping in my lower abdomen! I had to literally hold my hands over my stomach because of the pain. Meanwhile, the involuntary bowing motions continued. By this time, I had a little more understanding about physical manifestations. About a week and a half before the nine-month anniversary service, I had developed sharp back pains and abdominal cramping while Steve Hill was preaching. I know he noticed the expression of pain on my face, but I think after a few minutes he knew it was a physical manifestation.

Somehow I knew the pain was spiritually derived, so I stayed in the sanctuary in spite of the pain. Whenever I had to stand up, I held my sweater over my abdomen for comfort's sake, and for a minute I got lost in dealing with the pain and awkwardness. I knew it was physically impossible for me to be pregnant, but those pains sure felt like pre-labor pains (a mother never forgets what they feel like). I told my girlfriend about the pains a few times during the message and afterward, but neither of us made a big deal out of it. The following Sunday my girlfriend and I heard a lady moaning in the sanctuary before the service began. When Steve Hill came out he explained that an usher's wife was spiritually giving birth to the fruit of the revival that had been going on for almost nine months. I elbowed my girlfriend, and we both smiled. We both knew at that point that I too had experienced the pre-labor pains of that spiritual birth earlier that week.

Manifestations of God's Movement

I knew the God of the Bible often worked in pictorial types, shadows, and symbolism. The Old Testament shows how He demanded careful and intricate obedience to His defined patterns. This is why my first experience with "spiritual labor pains" didn't phase me. It made perfect sense to me that God would create, work through, and require the same kinds of shadows, patterns, and pictorial communication with His people in such a mighty end-time revival.

Now, however, God seemed to be blending together this bowing and the labor pains. I didn't give much thought to its meaning because it took all my strength and effort just to stand up. I received a greater understanding a few weeks later when Steve Hill explained to the congregation that intercessors today, as in almost every historical revival that has swept across a nation, often "give birth" to new souls in the spirit realm prior to their salvation. It was just a form of giving birth to new spiritual life.

In each service I attended for the next month or more, I experienced the same odd combination of being thrown into my pew during worship, receiving jolts of God's power like punctuated "amens" to key statements, and having the deep bowing and "pains" during altar calls. God also changed my prayer language (speaking in other tongues) from a fairly fluent tongue into a fervent but undeveloped tongue that resembled stammering. Although I had often been led of the Spirit to speak in an "unknown tongue over the years," this was different in that I had absolutely no control over my mouth.

After a week or so, I didn't care what anyone else thought about the way God's power was affecting me. I was too exhausted from keeping up with God to care. I didn't have the time, the energy, or the desire to question any manifestations around me either. In a lot of ways, God made me become pliable clay in His hands through all of that.

During the next few weeks, I felt the Holy Spirit lead me to start "marching" when people came forward. At other times I was instructed to "wave them down to the altar." At times I also felt an urgency to make a beckoning motion to the heavens as God sent down a special anointing to His people. In retrospect, it seemed like I was praying to God with hand motions or by acting out things that needed to occur in the natural or spiritual world. At first, I really had to stay focused on God to sense what the Spirit was leading me to do, but later I relaxed and was able to flow with greater confidence and overwhelming joy. God seemed to add one or two additional types of prayer hand motions every couple of weeks. I know one thing for sure: I certainly wasn't making those things up.

Complete Obedience to God's Call

You might be thinking that I've stepped "out there in left field somewhere," and I can understand the doubts you may have. However, I think the Bible offers an interesting perspective to all this. Are these actions of yielding our bodies in intercession really any more radical or unusual than the obedience of hundreds of thousands of Jews who marched around the walls of Jericho for six days, blasted a trumpet, and shouted at the defenders?[1] What about Gideon? He obeyed the Lord and did the exact opposite of what human thinking would dictate when he reduced his army from 22,000 men to only 300. In the end, God gave him the victory over the massive army of Midianites using an arsenal that consisted of only clay pitchers, oil lamps, trumpets, and loud shouting. (What would the critics call Gideon today?)

And the three companies blew the trumpets, and brake the pitchers, and held the lamps in their left hands, and the trumpets in their right hands to blow withal: and they cried, The sword of the Lord, and of Gideon. And they stood every man in his place round about the camp: and all the host ran, and cried, and fled (Judges 7:20-21).

God has His own way of doing things. Who are we to question Him? In our modern world, we think we are too sophisticated for such intricately defined obedience. However, I found that once I became personally intimate with Him and experienced manifestations of His power in my life, then obedience and yielding to Him on a moment-by-moment basis came more naturally. I began to understand that He uses even the smallest acts of obedience to fulfill His purposes through me and others. I believe the experience of being "jolted" by His power freed me from being controlled by the opinions of man. It also freed me from the limitations that I had unknowingly placed on God.

As God began to use me in other forms of intercession in the months to come, I began to wish I could just go to church and "mellow out" sometimes. It took effort and focused obedience to concentrate on the Spirit and yield myself to what the Spirit was doing. Whenever I felt that familiar "whininess" coming on, I reminded myself of Ezekiel, who laid on his left side for 390 days and ate and drank precisely what the Lord said by exact measurement. Then he rolled over to his right side and did the same thing for another 40 days!²

God obviously wanted to make a dramatic point through the obedience of His prophet. It is also clear that Ezekiel had to be close to God to obey a request involving such a great personal sacrifice. Ezekiel's relationship with God made it possible for the prophet to obey regardless of what people thought about his outlandish actions. Now you understand why "whininess" usually leaves me the moment I remind myself of Ezekiel and other brave servants of God in the Bible.

Many months later God proved to me the power of intercessory prayer in a very concrete way. During a Saturday night service, I sensed a "spirit of warfare" (marked by an urgent need to pray with supernatural authority and urgency) come upon me at the very beginning of the song service. I began to pray fervently in my prayer language (praying in other tongues). I also began to make hand motions as if I was cutting through something. This went on during most of the service. I knew I was definitely "out of the flow" with everyone else because most people were jubilantly praising the Lord in song and worshiping Him (which is probably what they were *supposed* to be doing, just as I was anointed to intercede in that service).

I kept quiet and prayed silently during the short evangelistic message, but my spirit was restless. I still felt the urgency to conduct spiritual warfare against "something" I couldn't define or describe. When the altar call was given (and the level of volume in the auditorium increased as well), I broke into prayer in tongues of warfare.

During most of the service, I received some hard looks from a couple of people who seemed shaken by my actions because they seemed so "out of order." I really believe in doing all things "decently and in order," and I would never consciously disobey or dishonor those in authority over me. However, I had to obey the Spirit's leading that night. I knew my actions were not out of order in the eyes of Pastor Kilpatrick or Brother Steve Hill because they would have immediately dispatched an usher to stop my actions if they sensed I was out of line. No, I just had to fight through the opinions of man to obey the Spirit that night. At the end of the altar call I turned to my girlfriend and commented, "I sure would like to know where all this warfare is going and where the opposition is coming from!" I didn't have to wait long for my answer. It came the very next morning.

At the beginning of the Sunday service, Pastor John Kilpatrick came out and asked his wife, Brenda, to come up on the platform. Then he said, "Last night we had to close off the back of the church and shut down the air conditioning because someone had ignited a toxic gas bomb in the church. A bomb of the same type was also released at a grocery store nearby. The people at the grocery store became very ill when they breathed the fumes from that bomb, but praise God, no one here at the church became ill last night!"

After the applause died down, Pastor Kilpatrick said that on his way home from church last night, a car ran through a stop sign and could have easily hit him. Then he smiled and said he had sailed through the situation without a scratch! That was enough for me. I broke into tears. This was an absolute confirmation that God had used me to conduct warfare for His people in Spirit-led prayer in other tongues. I didn't know how to pray or even what I was praying for, but the Spirit knew how to pray through me—all He needed was an obedient vessel. I was thankful to God for giving me such a timely confirmation of the victory that had been won in the Spirit.

Then Pastor Kilpatrick asked Brenda, who has always reminded me of a petite little blonde girl with loads of wisdom behind all her sweetness, to tell the congregation about a confrontation she had had the night before! She told us of a man who had come at her to verbally harass her after a ladies' meeting. She boldly proclaimed the name of Jesus and claimed the victory. She testified she had received a great boldness from God through the anointing she had received during the revival.

I cried through the rest of the service, even during Pastor Kilpatrick's message. I was overcome with thankfulness that God had helped me hold my ground and do exactly what I knew the Holy Spirit had asked me to do. Now I had learned that my obedience had in some way helped bring protection and the fruit of victory to my church and to the lives of my pastors. Someone on the outside of the situation might be tempted to minimize the correlation, but the matter was settled in my mind and heart. This experience gave me a deeper understanding of the love of God for me, and of my role in His Kingdom.

Open Doors for a Yielded Vessel

Many things occurred between the spring of 1996, when God began revealing gifts of intercession in me, and the fall of 1996, when He began to bring those gifts into fruition. Just prior to the April 1996 Pastors' Conference, I asked Rose Compton, Pastor Kilpatrick's administrative assistant, if I could contact a couple of magazines about doing an article on the conference. She recommended that I contact the Assemblies of God magazine,

The Pentecostal Evangel. When I called the editor, he asked me to write a short article on the conference for them.

The task of writing the article allowed me the privilege and benefit of attending all the sessions of the pastors' conference, which are normally limited to registered pastors and their wives. Although there were about 1,500 pastors and their wives at the conference, a close spirit of intimacy and unity permeated the whole conference. The sessions began on Tuesday night with a teaching by Brother Dick Reuben. Brother Reuben is known around the world for his expertise in the Jewish Tanakh (the Old Testament), and for his powerful teaching ministry using full-scale reproductions of tabernacle furniture and the priestly garments of Aaron. He taught the pastors about the golden altar in the tabernacle of old. He carefully reenacted the actions of the ancient priests, and as he put burning incense on the altar, he described the meaning of each kind of incense. Afterward, he asked all the pastors to come forward and throw incense on the golden altar as a representation of putting all their pain at the feet of Jesus.

Tears flowed from the eyes of most of the pastors and their wives as they filed back to their seats, and many remained quiet and introspective most of the conference. Many women shared with me that they had come to the conference deeply scarred from hurts that had been inflicted on them by the spiteful words of people in their churches. They said that God was pouring healing oil into their hearts during the conference, and one pastor's wife said she felt her fear of what people think just lift off of her shoulders. A few months later, I spoke with her and she shared that she had returned to her church and was able to speak in front of the whole congregation for the first time in her life! We heard many testimonies of how large numbers of souls were saved and how the Spirit of holiness and anointing had powerfully fallen in many of these pastors' churches when they got back home. My most intimate and treasured memory of that conference, however, will always be the overpowering love I felt for these men and women of God.

I also had the first of several divine appointments at the conference when I met Janet Young, a missionary sponsored by Brownsville Assembly of God. We met during one of the morning sessions and decided to have lunch together. There were only a few seats available where lunch was being served, and Janet asked if I wanted to sit at a spot to the left, but I instead pointed to the right and said I thought for some reason we were supposed to sit there.

Several minutes later, I started making small talk with a gentleman sitting across from me. When he learned that I was doing a little writing on the conference, he said, "Well then, I know someone you ought to meet: This is Jerrell Miller, the editor of the *Remnant* newspaper." I talked briefly with Jerrell and learned that the *Remnant* was a monthly "revival" publication with a small circulation on the Gulf Coast. It was also distributed monthly at the revival. He said that he thought Brownsville Assembly needed to think about beginning their own publication, and I told him that I had been talking with the church office about doing just that. He said over and over that he knew in his spirit that I was definitely called to do the job. Janet remarked afterward, "That was a divine appointment if I ever saw one." I didn't realize what my discussion with Jerrell Miller would lead to, but I was glad I had yielded to the Spirit and sat where He led me.

One of the most awesome components of the conference was the privilege of attending a session taught by Ruth Ward Heflin. Her message gave me a hunger to press into the glory of God. I longed to enter the spiritual place where I could become one with the Spirit of God. After that meeting I also pressed in to hear the voice of God more often.

Glorious Freedom in God

Now I know that at the onset it doesn't seem like looking and listening for the Spirit would be required if God truly wants to give you those things, but I can tell you from personal experience that a person can get spiritually lazy. Hearing the voice of God and seeing visions takes a lot more concentration than "hanging out" in praise, worship, and prayer. Sister Heflin motivated me out of my complacency and challenged me to press in for more than I already had. She had written a book entitled *Glory*, and that was the first book I read that was distributed from the revival.[3]

After I began reading *Glory*, I started conducting spiritual warfare in my house while dancing to the Lord to the rich sounds of Brownsville and Vineyard worship music. One of the key Scriptures Sister Heflin presented in her book highlighted the battle David won through song, praise, and dance before the Lord:

And when [David] *had consulted with the people, he appointed singers unto the Lord, and that should praise the beauty of holiness, as they went out before the army, and to say, Praise the Lord; for His mercy endureth for ever. And when they began to sing and to praise, the Lord set ambushments against the children of Ammon, Moab, and mount Seir, which were come against Judah; and they were smitten* (2 Chronicles 20:21-22).

I found it absolutely amazing how, through singing and dancing before the Lord, I would be instantly freed from every trace of oppression, depression, fear, or anxiety that rose up to attack me each day. Whether the attacks came from men or from the dark realm, I would just put on a worship tape and imagine myself dancing right over the top of whatever oppression was trying to attack me as I sang God's praises and danced before Him.

After I sang and danced with my daughter Aimee a few times, I found myself freely waltzing while I thought about the marriage supper of the Lamb, or while I'd envision myself in church helping to change the atmosphere there from one of stiff resistance to one of freedom to dance and express love for Jesus.

After a few weeks of this, I obeyed the burden to walk down almost to the front of the far right aisle of the church. Then I allowed the Spirit to move me to waltz in place to a song about the marriage supper of the Lamb. Before that, I had only been able to jump up and down in church, but now I really had the freedom to waltz in place before the Lord. Again, God was gently nudging me to do what was pleasing to Him with less and less concern for what people thought. By His mercy, He was tenderly freeing me step by step to praise and worship Him while I interceded for others. He was freeing me to do what I was created to do—give Him praise and please Him. The angels in Heaven declare, "Thou art worthy, O Lord, to receive glory and honour and power: for Thou hast created all things, and for Thy pleasure they are and were created."[4]

After I received more encouragement from the book *Glory*, I began to regularly dance and pray as I entered into the presence of God. First I would enter His courts with praise, then I approached Him in a spirit of worship, and finally I came to the spiritual place of hearing the still, small voice of God's guidance and of seeing visions.

There are pastors and others who wish their churches would suddenly be blasted with the things they see at Brownsville, such as jubilation, dance, intimate worship, souls being won en masse to the Lord, etc. I have often heard Steve Hill and Pastor Kilpatrick ask these persons if they are *really* ready for revival. I was blessed to be in a church where the freedom and gifts God gave me were not smothered. I was blessed to be in a place where the pastor dances and jogs around on the platform regularly and where his sweet wife can nightly be seen bowing in intercession or dazed under the glory blanket of God.

I believe God wants us all to be free of dead religion and, in this new dispensation, to be like David, Deborah, Elijah, Ezekiel, Peter, and Paul. There was a time when I said I was pressing in for an anointing that would be so powerful that my shadow would heal the sick like Peter's did. Steve often uses that phrase to keep himself and the rest of us humble. However, I now just want to see His face and be able to hear His voice. I want to see where the Spirit is moving in my mind's eye so that I can be instant in obeying Him.

Sharing the Revival

Near the end of the spring of 1996, my mother, who lives in Kentucky, invited me to go to a family reunion. It seemed like every opposition came against me to keep me from going, so I decided it was too much of a hassle for it to be God's will. The night before we were supposed to leave, my daughter Aimee asked me to read her a book. Out of 200 books in our home, she came in with one called, *I Don't Want to, God*. I chuckled to myself at God's unique ways of guiding us when the book turned out to be about a bunny who didn't want to go to a family reunion but ended up having a great time. I got the message. We left the next day.

At the reunion my mother introduced me to a cousin I had never met who was a pastor. She said, "Zack, this is my daughter Renee. She goes to the Brownsville church in Pensacola." He almost dropped his soda and immediately had me sit down with him because he wanted to talk with me about the revival. I told him I thought the revival was rooted in prayer, and he asked me if I would speak on prayer at his church the following night. Then he waved over another cousin I had never met who was an Assemblies of God pastor. Both of these cousins had taken their families and sent a lot of church members to Brownsville in recent months. Needless to say, we had a lot to talk about.

It all took me by surprise because while at the revival, I had developed a bit of sadness about not having any relatives with roots in the ministry like so many other people. After this, I would have lots of company down in Pensacola, Florida. Seriously, though, the family connection I felt was so strong that it seemed like we had grown up together in the natural and now we were growing up together in more of the fullness of what God had for us in these last days.

When I started talking to people the next night at my cousin Zachary Strong's church in Paducah, Kentucky, I found out I was the guest speaker for the evening. Fortunately, when I had sought God regarding what to cover, He had given me a lot of things to say.

I spoke about how my prayer life had changed. Many came forward to commit to walking closer to the Lord than they had ever before considered. One family, who had backslid, came up for salvation. A woman called the next morning and asked me to speak at a prayer meeting the following day. The group of about ten women seemed relieved to hear that there was more in God than they had experienced so far. One woman said, "I knew there had to be more. I just knew it. And now that I've heard what you have to say, I know it for sure." Then she broke into tears.

That day I called Pastor Kilpatrick's administrative assistant, Rose Compton. I told her that if she heard through the grapevine that I was speaking without authorization, it was all true. I told her to tell Pastor it was a family thing. She told me that it was good I called. It seemed I went from one ministry meeting to another that week. Tuesday night I led a prayer meeting similar to the one held on Tuesdays at Brownsville. On Wednesday night I spoke at my other cousin's church, Concord Assembly of God, and God just took control of my words and led me to speak on revival starting in individual hearts and lives and spreading outward. My daughter Rachel also testified about how God had changed her life from one of religion to one of being on fire for Jesus. I was so very proud of her.

When my cousin, Robert Strong, asked everyone to come forward for me to pray over them I thought, *Uh oh, I've never done this before.* People were lined up for prayer across the front of the altar. I put my hand on the forehead of the first one and thought, *Well, here goes, Lord.* I was surprised (and very relieved) when she fell over backward. After that, about half the people I prayed for fell over backward. Others dropped to their knees crying. Rachel prayed for the young people, and I think most were slain in the Spirit.

When we returned to Pensacola two weeks later, summer had begun. It was a time for waiting hours in long lines to get into the church, but mostly it was time to go to work.

Endnotes

1. See Joshua 6:1-17.

2. See Ezekiel 4:1-17.

3. Ruth Heflin, *Glory* (Shippensburg, PA: Destiny Image Publishers, 1990).

4. See Revelation 4:11.

Chapter 10

Time to Go to Work

Few of us got much sleep during the weekend of the Father's Day celebration at Brownsville. It was the revival's one-year anniversary. The crowds began to line up outside every door as early as 10:00 a.m., hoping for a seat in the sanctuary for the 7:00 p.m. services leading up to the big day. At the time, I didn't know that it was a preview of how long the lines would be that whole summer.

At exactly 5:00 p.m., ushers equipped with walkie talkies were posted at each of the five doors leading into the sanctuary. Everyone's adrenaline rose higher and higher as we waited for the signal. The crowds pressed closer and closer into the doors as the seconds were counted down. Sweat dripped down our backs, and our feet were swollen from standing so long. We were barely able to breathe, but we stood our ground, placing one foot forward as if we were at the start of a foot race. We were used to sweaty bodies pushing up against us and people stepping on our toes these last few minutes before the doors finally opened. We weren't going to get stuck in the chapel and watch the service on the large-screen television. We were determined to get into the sanctuary and that was all there was to it.

At last the radio call came. Bill Bush, the head usher, led the charge: "Open the doors!" The ushers took a deep breath, and at the crack of the doors the crowds burst past them. The ushers tried to contain the subdued frenzy by repeating, "Walk, walk." Oftentimes I didn't have to walk because the momentum of the crowd practically lifted my feet off the ground and jet-propelled me into the sanctuary. I usually grabbed the first seat I saw because anyone who was picky usually ended up with no seat at all and would find themselves in one of the overflow rooms watching the service via television.

One time as I was coming in I was walking up the aisle to the front of the sanctuary. I had heard that Brownsville people were lining up at the back door and getting in a few seconds earlier than people who hadn't figured it out yet. I entered with this group. When I walked up, the front doors had just been opened and it looked like a tidal wave of bodies surged in and devoured every chair in its path.

A Place in the Body

In retrospect I've considered that I should have given my seat to visitors who were coming from all over the country and around the world just to go to the revival for a few days. In fact, a lot of Brownsville people stayed home on revival nights to do just that. Once in a while I would overhear people say they voluntarily gave up their seats to visitors and went into the overflow rooms.

However, there were some Brownsville people who knew they were called to be in the sanctuary when they could get in because it was important that not everyone there be visitors. They went to assist with the flow of the anointing, intercession, singing, etc. I knew my main job at the time was to minister freedom of praise and worship to visitors. That was confirmed to me just a few days after I had "waltzed in place" for the first time. A young woman came up to me and asked me to pray for her. However, I explained that I couldn't because I wasn't on the prayer team. (This team has been carefully trained to counsel people who come forward for salvation and have been released to pray for people under the pastoral authority of Pastor Kilpatrick and the church leadership.) Tears welled up in her eyes and she said, "Oh, no, can't you do that just this once?"

Again I told her I couldn't, and I said I was surprised by her request. Then she explained, "I watched you during the whole song service, and I wish so much that I could have just a little bit of the joy that you have. I wish I could have some of the closeness I see you have with the Lord." She started to cry again. I explained to her how I had fallen in love with Jesus. Then I encouraged her to read the book, *Glory*, and to get our intercessory prayer leader's tape series and manual. Many women who visited the revival would come up to me each week and tell me how blessed they were by me, and others said I was the first person they looked for when they came back to visit—even though they had spoken with me before. In spite of this constant confirmation and affirmation, I remained careful to never move beyond clapping and singing into dance unless there was an unction of the Holy Ghost.

There is one time that I make an exception to that guideline, and that is when I am not feeling very victorious. In those times, I force my flesh and my soul to break out of the oppression by jumping up and down. Pastor Kilpatrick encourages us on a regular basis to "shake stuff off of us." I tell you, time and time again when I have jumped up and down to songs like "Look What the Lord Has Done," within the first few lines of the song, I break out of the doldrums and end up rejoicing before the Lord from the bottom of my heart. If we just take a step toward joy by faith, God will pour it on us in greater measure than we would ever think to ask.

By the time the Father's Day Sunday service rolled around, we were all so tired we could have been slain in the Spirit "without the Spirit"! The first man in line that morning set up shop at 4:00 a.m., hoping to get a seat in the sanctuary for the 10:00 a.m. service. Members were given tickets so they could get in earlier than visitors. My newfound elderly relatives who came down for the event from Kentucky that week barely made it in even though they ended up at the front of the visitors' line because of disability. We all knew one thing for sure: We were in for a memorable service!

Father's Day was just as it should have been. It was a time of "having breakfast with the family," only now I was part of the Brownsville Assembly family. The message was very important to me personally because it confirmed some things I knew to be true in my spirit. Yet all in all, it was really just "Dad" (Pastor Kilpatrick) talking to the kids. He thanked everybody in the family who had worked so hard during the past year of revival. Pastor Kilpatrick said the church family had been extra careful not to lift up the day (the one-year anniversary of the revival) like it was a man-made feast day. That just made me more thankful for the wisdom and discernment of the leadership of the Brownsville church.

That weekend I felt a strong burden from the Lord to apply for approval to be on the prayer team, and I turned in my application. That week Jerrell Miller from the *Remnant* newspaper came up during a mid-week service and asked if we had gotten the Brownsville publication off the ground. I told him I hadn't heard a response on the idea yet. Then he asked me to write a column for him. Again he told me he felt sure I was called to write about the revival. Of course, I agreed to write the column even before he gave me any of the details. Before walking off, he said I could write about anything I wanted and that I needed to send him a picture of myself to go with the column. I had no idea what doors would end up opening for me after this.

I wrote my first column in July. It was about how God had transformed Rachel from a drifting teen to a fired-up teenage evangelist. It also told how my home had become a teenage outreach center. Overnight the heat went up and the spotlight came on. I saw people look at my picture in the *Remnant,* look up at me, and then back down at the paper again. Hundreds of people came up to comment on the column. I did not like the attention, but I got used to it. After that, nearly everyone I met at any church in town would say something like, "Hey, you're the one with the picture in that paper. I've been reading your column."

My interview for the prayer team came on Friday night, two weeks after I had turned in my application. A panel of three people questioned me about my church background and my walk in Christ. I told them I had done just about every type of church work imaginable over the past 14 years. I also told them I had backslidden after an emotional crisis. I shared that I had been in the revival for six months and would never knowingly do anything that would bring shame to Christ. They said they would let me know their final decision within two weeks, and they said Pastor Kilpatrick had to personally approve all the applications for the prayer team.

Just two days later, on Sunday afternoon, Jeanie Bush, the prayer team coordinator, called me and said she was happy to tell me that I had been approved for the team. She said that although I had signed up for Friday nights, I could start praying on Wednesday night. Those hours I spent standing at the back door before each service turned out to be a great time of fellowship with other members of the prayer team. We would talk, then sing for a while. Periodically we would become tired and be comfortable just being quiet together.

Joining the Work of Revival

That first night before I was to pray with the team, the mother of one of Rachel's friends encouraged me not to be nervous about being on the team for the first time. She and her husband always pray right up front under the pulpit. She said a lot of people didn't like to pray there because it's so crowded and so much work, but she and her husband like it there. She said praying there takes a little getting used to because the team leaders are right there watching everything you do, but she didn't mind that. "Some nights it seems like everyone you pray for goes right down, and then some nights it seems like no one does and you wonder what in the world is wrong with you," she said. "Don't worry about it when they don't go down. It's not anything with you; it's whether or not the people you're praying for are open."

That first night I went into the room where the prayer team meets each night for a few minutes before the service.

Members of the team meet there every night to pray at 6:30 p.m. Jeanie, the coordinator, welcomed me sweetly before the others arrived and gave me my badge. I sat next to my friend who had encouraged me earlier. She treated me a little like I was her daughter. I went to the bathroom at the last minute and ended up making a spectacle of myself when I walked in and the leader for the night said, "There she is," and had me introduce myself as a new member of the team. The room was packed.

I raised my hand when they asked if anyone didn't have a partner. An older lady agreed to pair up with me. Since I was new I received first pick on the location in the church where I was to pray. I picked front and center, right under the pulpit. I figured I needed all the help I could get from the prayer team captains who would be overseeing me. I really felt a part of the team.

Steve suddenly entered and we all joined hands so that each person was connected. Steve gave us a brief pep talk about there being a lot of people out there that night who needed prayer. He said he knew that some of us in that room may have already had a hard day at work or at home, and that we might be feeling there was no way the anointing could flow through us that night. He said it didn't matter whether we felt anointed or not, because the anointing comes from God, not from us.

He then confidently and boldly prayed for the Lord to send in the power of His Spirit to set the captives free and heal the sick and brokenhearted. He briskly walked out of the room as quickly as he entered. As he left he shouted, "More, Lord!" We all smiled at one another, and I felt like someone should hike a football. (God bless Steve Hill—we need a thousand more just like him!)

When I walked into the sanctuary to find my seat, everyone was already standing up, and the song service was underway. I walked past a few people I knew who immediately noticed my new purple prayer team badge. Each of them gave me a congratulatory smile.

My first duty was to counsel people after the altar call. I talked with a young girl to be sure she understood what salvation meant and exhorted her to find a strong church and read her Bible and pray daily. I also prayed with her. Then I found my prayer partner. We positioned ourselves under the pulpit. I could only remember a few of the phrases we were allowed to say, so I mostly said, "More, Lord." The first person I prayed for fell backward very quickly. I was glad when people went down right away because it seemed to quickly affirm that they had received something. By the time I was a veteran a few nights later, I no longer cared whether or not they went down. I was praying with a major veteran, Gary Hinckey, who limited his prayers to about 30 seconds and just moved right along, acting as confident as could be that they had all received something whether they fell backward or not. From that night on, I pretty much moved right along in the same way.

The next night I realized that signing up to pray on Friday nights really meant signing up to pray every night. Each night Bill Bush would come out at 6:30 p.m. and announce that more prayer team members were needed and that all members needed to go to the meeting in the back. After a while I just went back there automatically. By the third week, I was so exhausted from concentrating on praying for people and catching people who fell backward on me that I was in tears by the end of the night. Gary Hinckey, the brother who showed me how to pray for people without worry, told me I had to commit to taking one night a week to get prayed for and receive from the Lord, even when they called for more team members.

New Lessons and Greater Visibility

About three weeks after I had become part of the prayer team, Pastor Kilpatrick asked all the prayer team members to sit on the platform. Sitting up there the first time was totally weird. First, I was looking at the faces of the people in the congregation instead of at the backs of their heads. (That night, the church actually looked much smaller than it had seemed when I was baptized.) Second, it was strange to be sitting so close to Pastor John Kilpatrick and Steve Hill. Third, singing and trying to freely move around while praising the Lord was impossible because, although I knew probably no one was looking at me, I knew they could if they wanted to. Fourth, looking at the back of Steve's head while he preached was very odd. Fifth, I was afraid to scratch my nose for fear of distracting someone from the message.

In other words, I did not like it at all, but like everything else, I became used to it. I also learned how to work around sitting up there for the whole service on the nights the choir wasn't singing and the prayer team was requested to sit up there. I simply looked for a spot off to the side of the sanctuary so I could go down and more freely jump up and down, dance, and intercede during worship. Then I would go back up and sit on the platform with the other prayer team members during the message.

Early on, I realized that the focus of my life was narrowing. One night I offended a lady who was saying that her husband, a pastor, had given a message after Hurricane

Opal in which he exhorted the congregation that the belongings they lost had been only temporary things. I told her that after-the-hurricane messages like that had really hurt me because I needed people to support me and let me grieve over the loss of my home. She and I went back and forth a bit about it.

Well, it turned out that her husband had died a few months after giving that message and she had been trying to reminisce about what a good preacher he was. I felt like I should be given the "smart mouth" award. I profusely apologized to her under the watchful eye of everyone else in the bathroom. I felt like I had just stepped into a bear trap, but I knew it was a revelation of a serious heart condition, and the Lord was calling me to take greater care when speaking of my testimony.

After that incident, when I went up and sat in the choir loft with the other prayer team members, I felt like I had the word *sinner* stamped across my forehead. I vowed to the Lord to watch my mouth like never before.

In the fall of that year, my daughter Aimee's teacher had her fill out a questionnaire about herself. One of the questions on the form asked, "What did you do this summer?" Aimee had filled in the blank: "I went to revival!" I burst out laughing because for the rest of our lives we will indeed always remember the summer of 1996 as just that: "We went to the Brownsville Revival."

We'll remember the sweat from standing in line. We'll remember the many people we met and said good-bye to. We'll remember Steve's love for souls. We'll remember Pastor Kilpatrick's happy face. We'll remember Sister Kilpatrick going along with her husband's loving jokes about how naively trusting she is. We'll remember Lindell hopping around and making outrageous faces while he tries to get every ounce of nourishment out of each chord. We'll remember the twinkle in Steve's eye when he got his wife Jeri up on the platform and teased her about not hogging the microphone. We'll remember the comfort of hearing Brother Rueben's powerful voice echo around the sanctuary when he bellowed out the prayer, "Now!" We'll remember the love in the eyes of Brother Richard Crisco when he looks at his brood of young people all vying to snatch just a moment of his time. We'll remember the safety we felt knowing the children were under the care and instruction of Pastor Vann.

We'll remember Brother Robertson saying, "For those of you who think you don't need to be baptized because the thief on the cross never did, you have two choices: You can either die on the cross or get in the baptismal pool." We'll remember Dr. Michael Brown, who joined the team late in the year as dean of the new ministry school, gritting his teeth and saying "Fill!" as he so intently prayed for us. We'll remember the unity we felt working together in our assigned places as ushers, table workers, choir members and singers, maintenance and cleaning crews, deliverance team members, cameramen, soundmen, intercessors, greeters, office and staff workers, youth and children's workers, security guards, and prayer team members, just to name a few.

And of course, we'll remember young Charity James, who night after night belted out the song, "Run to the Mercy Seat," as men, women, and children stormed down to the altar from every direction.

We'll remember the baptisms and the testimonies and lying on the floor under the peaceful presence or violent shaking of the glory of God while hordes of people stepped over our heads or fell on our feet. We'll remember our own tears and the tears of others as we learned the tenderness of our loving Savior. We'll remember the dancing. We'll remember the shouts and proclamations of victory.

We'll remember Lila Terhune, our intercessory prayer team coordinator, turning around in a circle in her pew while spinning her hand around over her head as she became taken up with intercession. We'll remember Rose Compton calmly ticking her way through every area of the church making sure everything was running smoothly. And maybe most of all, we will remember the tenderness and the challenges of bearing together as brothers and sisters in Christ, who were doing all we knew to do and looking to God to do the rest.

We'll also surely remember Brother Elmer flicking the lights for the tenth time each night, saying, "That's it, folks, it's time to go home." Sometimes I think, *I can't wait until I hear Brother Elmer in heaven say, "This is it, folks, we're home. You can stay put for eternity."* But until then, we've only just begun.

We still faced an exciting fall and winter season with the river of God and the fire of revival. We were to discover that even after our month-long break during December, 1996, the Spirit of revival was still there, just waiting for living vessels to receive God's glory anew in yet another miraculous year of power.

Chapter 11

Spreading the Good News

Fall of 1996 began with a battle cry for youth. Hundreds of teenagers marched up onto the platform, and at the sound of Brother Dick Reuben blowing the *shofar* (sheep's horn), thousands extended their hands toward these young people and shouted proclamations of victory in the name of Jesus. As the teens filed back to their seats, the whole sanctuary broke out in victorious, jubilant dancing.

Those fired-up teenagers stormed through their schools with a vengeance. My daughter Rachel and her friends Jill and Sarah, for example, shocked Gulf Breeze Junior High with the message of holiness. They had been waiting all summer for this. From the very first day of school, they walked around campus with their Bibles on top of their books. They wore T-shirts that boldly proclaimed Jesus Christ.

Everyone who saw them asked, "Why are you bringing your Bible to school, of all places?" The girls would seize each opportunity to tell the kids that they wanted to read their Bibles during every spare moment because Jesus was the most important thing in their lives. Rachel said that in those first few days absolutely everyone wanted to read the Christian statements on their T-shirts. Neither the students nor the teachers could believe their eyes.

After the novelty of their Bibles and T-shirts wore off, the persecution set in. These young believers were mocked and scoffed at, and some of the more aggressive kids started bringing in satanic bibles in an effort to oppose the Christian students. Usually it was the very kids who mocked them the most who ended up being the most interested and ready for change.

Young Soldiers in the Trenches

Within the first couple of weeks the girls formed a Bible club that met one morning a week for hard preaching and two mornings a week for prayer. (This is legal according to Florida law as long as the meetings are voluntary and the students have parental consent to attend.) They put up advertisements for the club around the school, and each of them witnessed to five to ten kids every day. They held their prayer meetings on the blacktop outside so all the kids waiting outside for school to start could see them. Some of the kids asked, "Why do you pray right out there in front of everyone?" Rachel responded by asking them, "Well, why do you cuss and swear right out there in front of everyone? I would much rather use my mouth for praying!"

Rachel was amazed at the number of kids who thought that going to church on Sunday made "everything all better" and made up for all of their "stuff that might not be so good." Those kids who went to church every Sunday were stunned when Rachel told them that they could only serve one of two masters—God or satan.

She told them the Bible required them to be saved by accepting Jesus Christ as their Savior *and* by repenting of sin, submitting to Him as *Lord* of their lives. Kids would just shake their heads and say, "Wow, I never knew that."

I couldn't help but think about how their churches and "yuppie" parents had failed these children for all these years. Now these kids were torn up and depressed. They were trying to find life and meaning in drugs, sex, and alcohol.

I couldn't help but think of all the suffering and violations these children had experienced by sitting in these churches Sunday after Sunday without anyone being bold enough to tell them there was a hell, and a devil, and that victory and freedom were available through Jesus Christ and through obedience to His Word. I thought of the tragedy after tragedy that stacked up across the nation and around the world. Then I thought of the other side of the coin. Some of Rachel's friends from her old private school attended churches that had laid so much religious bondage and oppression on them that they had already run away in their hearts because they had seen through the arrogance and hypocrisy.

God has said, "Enough!" He is raising up an army that is not ashamed. These soldiers are not ashamed of Him, and they are not ashamed of the gospel! He is raising up an army that knows Him, and because it knows Him, it is not afraid. He is raising up an army that is saying, "Yes, Lord, we will ride with You."

As winter approached, one of the ways these young soldiers of God recruited new attendants to come hear the gospel message at the junior high school was by going out where kids were sitting in the cold waiting for the school to open. Rachel and her friends would go outside and yell, "Hey, it's nice and warm in here where we're having Bible club."

Then, after they got the new kids inside, the Christian young people would tell the kids that they knew by their lives that they were not serving God. They would shoot straight from the hip, telling the kids that hell waited for all those who chose to live their lives their own way instead of accepting Jesus Christ and doing things God's way.

Rachel and Jill preached it hard and preached it straight during Bible club meetings. They challenged the kids about their language, their partying, their attitudes, their music, the television programs they watched, their promiscuity, their lying, their cheating, and on and on. Then they challenged these teens with holiness and the message of salvation through Jesus Christ.

One morning Rachel read the group a book about hell. Everyone shot their hand up for salvation that morning. Between 3 and 12 young people raised their hands for salvation after each meeting.

Rachel admits that at the beginning of the year, it was very hard. She and her friends felt like they were up against a stone wall, but as time passed it got easier and easier. I believe the girls won the respect of their peers, and their faith increased as they saw God move time and time again. Walls of oppression came down through their consistent prayers, and they gained strength in their new numbers.

Their greatest and most hurtful opposition came from the religious kids who wanted to challenge them with doctrinal claims to justify going to church and continuing their partying. These religious kids worked very hard to gang up on them and to turn others against them, even those who had never heard the gospel message.

I exhorted Rachel to never become roped into arguments about doctrine or church history. Rebellion against conviction of sin was at the bottom of this opposition. I encouraged her to pray for and be consistent with the kids who listened to the religious folks. In their hearts, even these listeners knew that they were vainly heaping up ammunition for their own rebellion. I told her to stand firm in her faith that God could break even the heaviest yoke of oppression and deception from off these young people and set their hearts free.

Growing in Strength and Numbers

Most of the new converts at school went to churches other than Brownsville, but they knit together for their unified purpose. They formed a discipleship program using the same materials as Brownsville's youth group. Rachel couldn't believe how committed the Bible group became to daily prayer, Bible reading, and sharing the gospel with others. The young people also committed to attending Bible and prayer meetings at school, fasting, maintaining journals, and memorizing Scripture. God not only used these young soldiers to win souls to Christ, but also to disciple them!

Rachel was excited to see how quickly many of the new Christians grew in the Lord. She rejoiced like a mother rejoices over the successes of her children. One day she kept saying over and over how she couldn't believe how committed some of the kids had become in such a short time. For example, she overheard one of the boys, who had been a Christian for only a few weeks, inviting another boy over to his house for a slumber party. The first boy said to the other, "You've got to come over Friday night because we're going to have a blast smashing all my rock 'n roll CDs in the backyard."

The storm that hit Gulf Breeze Junior High School was not a unique one. The same thing was happening at schools all around the county. News arrived daily of churches of every denomination in a city coming together for prayer and fasting, revival services, miracle healings, and deliverance. Churches were being set on fire with holiness and breaking out in freedom of worship. Pastors who had repented of complacency were now zealously burning for evangelism, altars full of repentant hearts and transformed lives. Bolts of the power of God were zapping preachers to their knees in the middle of church services. It was clear that God was moving and transforming His people.

In the months that followed, I personally was blessed with increased demands for writing. In the fall I was surprised by an opportunity that I thought had passed me by. I was asked to become the editor of the new Brownsville revival magazine, *Feast of Fire*. I was also given the privilege of writing this book, and I still get to talk straight from the heart in my monthly column for the *Remnant*.

Growing up is not always easy, and I often found myself longing for the days I could freely go to the revival just to soak in the presence of the Lord. Often when I was plugging away to meet a deadline, I found myself looking at my clock and calculating what was probably going on at the Brownsville Revival. I would think, *About now, they're having the break. Or now they're probably having the altar call...* I spent a lot of time alone with the Lord and with my children, and it seemed like I became more intimate with Him and with them each passing day. When I would grab a chance to go to the revival, I often found myself paralyzed under the blanket of His holy presence.

While I wrote this book, the enemy created many situations in an attempt to hinder me, but through these attacks I received an increased discernment of spirits. This increased discernment enabled me to better understand my rights as a child of God and my authority as a member of Christ's Kingdom. This understanding gave me greater freedom in the area of forgiveness of others because I learned to separate soul from spirit in my perspective and in my dealings with those trying to oppose the work of Christ. I was able to forgive the bondaged soul while warring against the spirits operating through him or her. This added understanding was also arming me for evangelism.

By the end of 1996, men and women of God from around the world testified of their new understanding of God's calling. They had never heard of that type of preaching before coming to the revival; the speaker at the revival boldly confronted sin. Now that they understood God's call to such holiness, they were committed to taking this message back to the people in their homelands who were hungry for God to touch their lives and their communities. God was on the move. From the Brownsville Revival, He was spreading the freedom that comes through holiness and intimacy with Him around the world.

Each night hundreds of ministers came as first-time visitors to receive "more of God" at the revival. These hundreds of ministers added up to many tens of thousands ready to take the anointing and message of holiness back to their churches across America and around the world.

People from every denomination and walk of life arrived in loaded buses, vans, and cars from every state in the nation. Large groups came from other countries as well. On any given night, as many as 15 to 20 countries would be represented. When Pastor Kilpatrick asked first-time visitors to raise their hands, usually at least 1,000, if not 2,000, raised their hands each night in the sanctuary alone.

When all those pastors in the November conference swooped down upon us like an infantry of soldiers equipped for battle, I knew it was harvesttime. I knew God was sending laborers into the field of the world to harvest souls for His Kingdom in these endtimes. What was happening at Brownsville was just a spark, and by His Spirit God was fanning the flame.

Continued Revival at Every Level

As 1996 came to a close and a new year of revival roared onto the scene, it seemed like God was picking up the pace and fanning His fire of revival to even higher heights! When Pastor Kilpatrick, Steve Hill, and other key participants in the revival met together in January after the break, they were of one mind and one accord: "God is going to continue His sovereign move in revival at Brownsville at least until the year 2000!"

On the home front, Rachel had become a discipleship leader under the guidance of Brother Richard Crisco. As I began this chapter, she sat across the kitchen table from me shaking her head, saying, "Mom, I just don't know what I'm going to preach on tomorrow [at the school prayer club meeting the following morning]." I looked at her and just said, "Thank You, Jesus!" How many mothers get to hear their teenage daughters say something like that?

The next day Rachel came running into the house and was jumping around in her excitement. She exclaimed, "Mom, 32 kids made decisions for Jesus Christ today at school!" Just before that my little Aimee had come to me and said, "Mom, I witnessed to five kids today!" Aimee told me that three of the five were boys who were "real tough kids." One of them told Aimee, "I don't need to worry about salvation because I go to church and was baptized." Aimee fired right back, "Well, you and I know your life, and if you're not living your life for Jesus, you can go to hell with baptismal waters on your face!"

Aimee also led an entire family to the Lord with the help of myself and another adult friend. First, she began to witness to the family. Then I witnessed to the mother. Finally, another lady came along and reaped the harvest when they all made a commitment to the Lord. This all happened the same week that Aimee witnessed to those five kids.

I immediately thought of Pastor Kilpatrick's message from the previous weekend. He had prophesied that in this revival God would raise up children to be evangelists. This was already coming to pass—not only in my house, but in the homes of countless families involved in the revival across the region and the world! These kids are incredibly bold once revival fire hits their hearts. One of the most exciting facets of this revival is that it is sweeping through *every* part of our church family. Pastor Vann Lane's ministry to the children manifests the same degree of supernatural power and visitations from God that the adults see in the main services! Richard Crisco's ministry in the youth services is marked by the same intensity seen in the main services, and at times, maybe even more. Churches and parents are busing in their kids from hundreds of miles away so the fire can ignite their hearts and change their destinies forever.

The people of Brownsville could literally fill a large room with the written reports that have come in of miracles, salvations, transformed lives, and the spreading of the fire of revival around the world. One of the most significant marks of revival is that when the glory of God falls on His people, one of the first things they feel is an intense concern and compassion for the lost. Time and time again, the Holy Spirit sovereignly turns the direction of the service toward seeking and saving lost souls. And prayer is at the heart of it all. Indeed, Pastor Kilpatrick reminds us again and again that humble, fervent prayer is what sustains this revival. Each day, week, and month we humbly ask God to send us revival again for one more day. We know all too well that true revival can only come from God.

Chapter 12

God Loves You and Has a Plan for Your Life

Every person who comes to the Brownsville revival has a story. No one encounters the river of God by accident. Somehow, somewhere, I know God's loving hand will show up in your life. He loves you and I so much that He sent His only begotten Son to salvage and save us. He also loves us enough to make sure we have every opportunity to "taste and see that the Lord is good."[1]

A Dream and a Hope

I don't know why you think you picked up this book, but I know the "who" behind it all. And I can only imagine that you wouldn't read this far through the book unless you had some type of hunger. Like me, you may be hungry for more of God. Before God transformed me at the Brownsville Revival, I was a Christian, but I was in the midst of a dark oppressive bondage. There was no escape in sight, but God shined a light of hope on me in Wichita, Kansas. He led me to move 4,000 miles in search of a dream based on those fleeting words, and He did this because He loved me.

God's Word declares that He is no "respector of persons."[2] He loves you just as much as He loves me, or Pastor John Kilpatrick, or Evangelist Steve Hill, or even the apostle Paul. For seven long years after I moved to Pensacola, I searched in vain for the revival God had told me about. I had lost all hope of finding His promised revival; but He moved Heaven and earth to plant me right in the midst of His glorious river of fire, and I have never been the same.

I have a strong sense that God has "moved Heaven and earth" for you too. I don't know your condition today, but I have had a personal experience with the power of God's river of life. In December of 1996, just before we temporarily suspended the revival services and entered our "holiday break," I wrote a column titled "God Loves You and Has a Plan for Your Life." I was working on this book at the same time I wrote the article, and a number of Brownsville people began to really encourage me. I felt a bit like I was running a race and all these wonderful people were along the sidelines rooting for me and handing me fresh drinks of water. I thought of many of them when I wrote that column and this chapter. The most important part of that column addressed the way God has worked out His plan in my life. Truly, there were no "accidents" involved in my move to Pensacola, just as it was no accident that you picked up this book.

God never ceases to surprise and challenge me. So many doors have opened for me to write that it is only by the grace of God that I have been able to keep up with everything over the past two months. These opportunities have been a Christian writer's dream come true, and I can only say that Jesus is showing me that God does really love me and always had a plan for my life.

Regardless of what happens in any current situation, God always has a plan. If one door closes for one reason or another, a better door will always open up as long as we remain faithful and "down on our face" in humility. This attitude is imperative for successfully knocking the lights out of fear and the idolatry of position when they rear their ugly heads.

A Calling for Each Person

Even before I knew what salvation meant, God called me to be a writer. Too many years ago to count, God spoke to my heart and told me to major in journalism. I was sitting in the courtyard of the junior college paging through a catalog that described all the degrees offered by California colleges and universities. I had decided to change my major from psychology to something less theoretical. Sitting on that bench by myself, I asked God what He wanted me to major in. His still, small voice said, "Public Relations."

I looked the topic up in the catalog and found that two colleges in California offered that major. San Diego State offered it in their Journalism Department, and Santa Barbara State offered it through their Business Department. I asked God which one I should go to, and He answered in that still, small voice, "Journalism." I actually didn't understand what Public Relations was until I moved to San Diego a few weeks later and started my classes. I simply knew what God had said and that was that.

I have always liked to write. As a child, I spent most of my time writing poetry at night rather than watching television. Even then, God was preparing me for the plan He had for me. However, I never wanted to be a starving poet, so I never considered becoming serious about writing.

Until the Brownsville Revival, I really didn't have anything to write about. I kept waiting for something to happen that was worth putting into print. I wrote for a weekly newspaper and did some newsletter editing and grant writing, but for the most part, I remained out of my field of study for too long to mention. I worked mostly as a business manager in various fields. However, I kept telling people I was going to be a writer, especially for about a year before the revival. I still didn't know what I was going to write about, but I knew I would write.

Later, during the revival, God brought me into the kind of intercessory prayer I described earlier, the kind of prayer that involved yielding my body to the moving of the Holy Ghost in a type of supernatural "prayer sign language." When the Holy Ghost led me to wave souls into His Kingdom or to motion the dividing of some spiritual Red Sea in front of His people, I could have resisted, but to resist made me feel like a person does who knows he or she is to witness to somebody and doesn't. It was awful, and I don't like feeling awful. I still don't know why God wants me to pray that way, but I guess it's for the same reason He wants us to pray at all—He just requires it, and it really doesn't matter if we understand it or not.

The same thing is true about writing. It's an obedience thing. Obeying the Holy Spirit from moment to moment in intercession was preparation for writing under the anointing. My descriptive writing style functions best when it is based on bare-bones humility and vision that only comes from God through prayer. I have found that is the kind of writing that makes people cry because it helps them to identify closely with how I felt. It is the kind of writing that is so self-revealing that people thank me for having the courage to write so honestly.

This type of writing is similar to intercession, for when I write under God's anointing, my mind is moved to that descriptive place where the Holy Spirit wants me to move, a place of description of feelings and impressions. It is a place I cannot go alone. This is much like yielding to the Holy Ghost as He bends me at the waist to bow before God under the weight of the Spirit, or like knowing from the way my heart leaps that it is time to jump up and dance before the Lord—even when no one else is doing it. It's all a matter of obedience. Without my obedience in intercession, the doors would not have opened for writing.

It Begins With You

Many of us have a heart for ministry. But we must ask ourselves: Are we willing to love the undesirables first? Are we willing to welcome guests even though we're tired? Are we willing to obey a burden to get up in the middle of the night and pray for souls and ministries? Are we willing to be broken and humbled in front of our peers? Are we willing to truly be a fool for Christ in witnessing, interceding, or testing? The list goes on and on. I will not say these are "little things" to be faithful in, for they are giving our lives as a part of our reasonable service.[3] That's why the list goes on and on.

The real challenge is to stay humble when God uses you, for that is the time you most need to stay humble. We succeed only by the grace of God and by personally pressing in for more holiness and more of Him. I well remember the pit from which I was dragged, and I know that the fight will only end when the Lord returns for His Bride. We will rest, yes. Slumber, no.

God loves you and has a plan for your life too. When I got in line behind Jesus and asked Him to wash away my sins in His blood and make me a new creature, I didn't know what was ahead. All I knew was that I was ready to follow Jesus. I was tired of trying to do it my way and making a mess out of my life and the lives of those around me. I simply surrendered to the fact that His way was better than mine. I decided to stop running from the truth and start drawing closer to it.

God knows about all your pain. He knows about all your confusion. He knows about all your feelings of un-worthiness. He knows about all the phoniness you've been hiding behind, trying to look good to others when, in fact, you're torn up inside. He is waiting tenderly, lov-ingly, and longingly for you to finally say, "At long last, Lord, I surrender it all to You. Not my will, but Thy will be done."[4]

God loves you and He wants revival to begin with you! If you want revival in your life, you can have it today. Per-haps, like me, you are coming to God with a heavy weight of mental or spiritual oppression pressing down on your shoulders and your future. You may be in the pit of de-pendency, hopelessly hooked on drugs, alcohol, sexual perversion, homosexuality, pornography, or even the ap-proval of men. Jesus Christ can set you free right now! Once He sets you free, He will keep you free by immers-ing you in His river of life. All you have to do is obey.

Thousands of people enter the doors of Brownsville Assembly of God each week carrying all the heavy bag-gage of their past failures, willful sins, and bitter hurts.

They come, like the man at the pool of Bethesda, hoping to step into miraculous waters and come out whole.[5] What they are finding is that God is no longer using stagnant pools that need to be constantly stirred. He is flooding Brownsville and other places around the earth with a mighty river of revival. For those who are willing to abandon themselves to God's river, there is freedom, healing, and forgiveness in the waters of God. I urge you to come to His fountain right now. Revival in your life and circumstances is only one step of obedience away! Fall on your knees and begin to pray. God will meet you there.

Endnotes

1. See Psalm 34:8.
2. See Acts 10:34.
3. See Romans 12:1.
3. See Luke 22:42.
4. John 5:2-9.